BODY DYNAMICS

Gertrude Enelow

BODY DYNAMICS

DRAWINGS BY IVAN WHITKOV

INFORMATION INCORPORATED

New York

To B. F. E.
*Whose wisdom and ideals will always be
an infinite source of inspiration*

ACKNOWLEDGMENTS

I wish to express my deepest gratitude to my students and the teachers in my school for their love, encouragement and dedication to Body Dynamics.

I wish also to acknowledge my grateful appreciation to Lilian T. Mowrer for her invaluable assistance and advice.

Contents

Preface

It is only when a mother has supreme confidence in a friend that she can relinquish her newborn child to be held, judged, and anointed by him; so is it also with an author who entrusts the product of her body and mind to the tender mercies of another. I am, therefore, deeply sensitive to Gertrude Enelow's act of faith when she asked me, a physician and psychoanalyst, to write a preface for her fascinating book.

The term *psychotherapy* stems from the Greek roots *psyche* and *therapeien,* meaning simply, service of that vital spark of immortal grace and creativity which man calls his *psyche* or "soul." But a classic Greek fable, concerning the beauteous maiden Psyche, presents a more deeply moving allegory; that of eternal youth yearning in the dark, true solitude of night for the embrace of no less than divinity and eventually enfolding in her arms the majestic, tender god Eros. As a physicist, the physician labors to avert all threats to man's bodily self-love or narcissism, but as a disciple of Psyche, he must also serve not only man's longing for human companionship but also his yearning for the touch of the immortal. And this, also, is the intent of this bodily-down-to-earth-reaching-for-a-friend-yet-stretching-to-the-stars volume.

But silent Narcissus, who admired only his own image, was changed into a mutely pining flower, whereas Psyche, although her dreams faded a little in the light of day, was honored for relating her wondrous experiences to her fellow-men. How then, shall we, too, explain psychiatrically—or, if you will, in biodynamic rather than in Body Dynamic terms —the more mundane magic of the calisthenics described in this manual?

Perhaps the essential secret, like all central truths, is pro-foundly simple. In effect, through the implications of Body Dynamics, we forsake the turmoil and stress of our cur-rently complex and complex-ridden existence and return to the healing wholeness (from Anglo-Saxon *hale*—healthy, whole, and holy) of the primal and the childlike. Much of this can be gathered from the enthusiasm of this volume, and more can be perceived as emanating from a group per-forming in unison the exercises here described—even though the subjective core of the experiences themselves can come only to one, who abandoning conscious inhibition, himself participates wholly in the procedures described. Then, and perhaps then only, can one vivify *existentially* i.e., with immediate personal significance—the merely intellectual ex-planations of his insights. However, since we are here con-fined merely to twisting words on separate strings, let us do what we can to separate the essences of Body Dynamics.

First, perhaps, is the emancipating and self-identifying experience of releasing the body from constrictive clothing, possibly also reminiscent of neonatal freedom. In Body Dy-namics classes the men and women wear appropriate clothing, displaying as much regard for bodily form—and as little concern for merely erotic preoccupations—as did Praxiteles when he sculptured his deathless tributes to unrestricted human grace in eloquent motion.

Second, and also appropriate, is the emphasis on *breathing*. It is often forgotten that the first contact of the newborn child with the universe outside is not with its mother's breast, but through its initial, engulfing breath—a revered event that is celebrated ever after in man's most profound and enduring conceptions. In the Latin tongue in which we still speak, breath is *spiritus*—and so the human *spirit aspires* to truth and beauty, is *dispirited* when unhappy or alone, and cultivates the *esprit de corps* of goodfellowship. Finally, when his body *expires*, man fancies his soul (Anglo-Saxon *sawol*, moving breath) as free to rejoin a holy spirit that knows no mortal limitations. Nor are these equivalences of breath, life, and immortality confined to our Roman-Gallic tradition. In the Indic Vedas, too, *hatma* means both breath, life and soul (a Mahatma is a Great Soul) and in Hebrew, *n'shama* has the same indissoluble connotations. When, then, Body Dynamics makes our very breathing an inspired prayer, this procedure alone evokes a resonance of aspirations that ranges from the most pristine to the most ethereal and transcendent.

Third is the author's profound intuition that, despite such flights of fancy, men really prefer to remain as close as possible to Mother Earth. One could imagine that the exercises described in this book would be most restorative were they performed whenever possible on a grassy sward, a bare rock, or an open sandy beach. However, since man insists on interposing artifices between himself and nature, Gertrude Enelow thus repeatedly directs: lie with your back in complete apposition to the floor, or, if you sit or stand, allow your spine, thighs or feet to feel as closely in contact as possible with what is fundamentally fixed beneath you. Even Hercules the demigod had difficulty with the giant Antaeus who, each time he touched the ground, not only healed his wounds but doubled his vitality and vigor. It is this feeling of symbolic reunion of man with his earthly origins to which a passage late in this book refers: "All the distinctions of the I and the not I are set aside."

Present in Body Dynamics too, is an intangible imprint, perhaps in the deepest layers of our atavistically Jungean consciousness, of our journey toward the sun through dim aeons of engulfing oneness with the warm, caressing, nutritive seas of our evolutionary infancy. Thus, many of the exercises here described recall the graceful waving of the flowerlike fronds of the marine anemone, the rhythmically sinuous motions of a swimming salamander, or the buoyant sea-larking dance of the dolphin.

But man is also a dependently gregarious animal, and his image of primal motherhood is not alone that of a womb-like antediluvian ocean, vast and impersonal. On the contrary, in man's wistful image, Mother Earth and her daughters are the epitome of individualized kindness and protection to the needy and the helpless. The recognition of this yearning, too, pervades the author's methods. For example, in her chapter on sleep, she counsels her pupils to "rest assured" in a lateral posture, like a child no longer huddled in the uterus, but nestled full length, protected and secure by the side of its mother. So also do later chapters dealing with the waking state recognize the semi-hypnotic nature of the directions and responses of Body Dynamics. Be it noted that hypnosis (misnamed after Hypnos, Greek god of sleep) is really neither sleep nor trance, but a relaxed communicant passivity significantly induced, as in Body Dynamics, by deep, regular breathing synchronized with elemental body movements done to the directions of a soothing, repetitious cadence, half-sung like a nursery lullaby. This results in the tentative, though never complete amenability of the regressed subject to the influence of his temporarily adopted and trusted mentor. Thus does Gertrude Enelow speak in her book—and thus she speaks even more directly, colorfully and intimately in her personally conducted classes.

Much, much more could be said about this little primer: about the walls of personal retreat which are built around some of the exercises, the furnishing of the private castle within those walls with the arts and crafts of fantasy, and each master's admission to his citadel only of those he finds sympathetic and congenial. And yet, when the company has been assembled, Gertrude Enelow advises all of them to stand on tiptoe in the courtyard and stretch their arms to an infinity about and above.

But the author's last chapter, aptly entitled "Stand and Face the World," places final emphasis on a sense of reality maintained throughout the book. Body Dynamics is not intended to be a cult for harried dreamers, or for frail poets, or for bored escapists seeking a new fad, or least of all for those deeply troubled by personal problems that need medical or psychiatric help. Instead, Body Dynamics is designed for practical men and women who wish to develop the inner strengths of their being so that they may perform and enjoy to the fullest their daily occupations, avocations and potentially richer familial and social relationships.

The alert and sophisticated will neither condemn these exercises nor yet give them a greater place than the author herself would accord them in the protean context of a fully rounded physical, intellectual and aesthetic life. It is to such discerning people that I commend this book—and Gertrude Enelow.

JULES H. MASSERMAN, M.D.

Chicago, January 20, 1960.

Introduction

The prime function of Body Dynamics is to make us more vividly conscious of reality—to rouse us from the half-sleep condition in which most of us pass through life. In Body Dynamics, your awareness and your spirit of adventure are wakened in the very first lesson. You receive benefits as soon as you start. You realize that full co-operation of all that is within you will bring the best and quickest results. You become conscious of the joy of perfecting yourself. You need no outside apparatus for this. You have all that you need, built within yourself. With beauty in your heart, you develop a new appreciation of your potentials and the God-given instrument that is you. You discover for yourself why Body Dynamics has brought so much to the lives of so many.

You learn how the correct sleeping position not only brings refreshing restful sleep but influences postural alignment as well.

You learn how a new kind of easy rhythmic breathing can increase your energy and your power when you need it.

You learn to shed the dead weight of your old self and to restore your suppleness, agility and youthful spirit.

You learn what strength there is in quietness—in no apparent activity.

You develop new controls that you can set against daily trivial irritations and annoyances.

You learn to go along with the natural rhythm of life rather than against it.

You perceive what it means to be alive in the universe.

You come to realize that you are a tangible reality, more remarkable than a jet or a missile; that you are the most remarkable and best put-together mechanism ever created. Since we are living in a time of expanding demands upon our energies and our nervous systems, we must have an understanding of the potential sources of energy in order to develop our creative resources on a scale never before possible.

We must prepare ourselves both mentally and physically to insure the future of what promises to be the most challenging decade in our history.

In America, especially, the growing insatiable demand for mechanical aids turns everything in our life today toward functionalism.

Body Dynamics is a unique method for the prevention of premature ageing and physical deterioration and protects the functionalism of the entire body.

The greatest efficiency of the human mechanism depends on using it as a complete unit and not just as an assembly of separate parts. For the highest possible strength and endurance, the body must function with unity. Every component part and every combination of parts must perform in harmony with the whole.

Everything within you has a special purpose. Even the

way you are put together indicates that the body was created to follow the natural lines of motion. When we get too far away from natural living and natural movement, we get off balance, set up tensions, squander our energies, and become indifferent to the body's needs. Our basic functions become distorted:

In sleep, we waken cramped and not rested.

In walking, we drag ourselves along.

In sitting, after a short time our backs ache.

We often feel as though we were made up of hundreds of aching parts, instead of feeling the power of body and mind unfolding as a single solid unit—in balance, in tune, in readiness to meet the strenuous demands of daily life. To use one's self with minimum effort as a complete whole requires careful training of the entire body. It takes patience, application and understanding to use the body with economy of effort and without strain in performing the most casual daily functions.

In my classes, people have been doing these movements for years. It is impossible within the scope of a book to present all aspects of Body Dynamics, but the basic elements that will enable you to achieve a more balanced mind and body have been set forth in the following pages.

G.E.

INCLUSION

Did you ever see a willow moving in a breeze
Swaying with the wind in freedom and ease?
Resistance is something the willow does not know
As it swings and it sings in the wind to and fro.

Did you ever see a stream rushing on its way
Gurgling most joyously all the long day?
It makes no difference where it is going.
Happiness lies in the joy of flowing.

Did you ever see a bird rising in flight
As with beauty of movement it wings out of sight?
'Tis enough to live these things to see,
And wonder if they are part of me.

G.E.

THE ZEN WAY

Empty-handed I go, and behold the spade is in my hands;
I walk on foot, and yet on the back of an ox
    I am riding.
When I pass over the bridge,
Lo, the water floweth not, but the bridge doth flow.

Famous saying of Jenye (Shan hui, A.D. 497)

1 Body Dynamics

What It Is All About

Man is born whole and can remain whole, but usually lives in a state of disharmony.

Every human being has capacities to do infinitely more than he does, were his energies only brought into focus.

For lack of adequate understanding and handling, the human mechanism grinds along spasmodically, underpowered and overburdened. Yet all the time, deep within ourselves below the threshold of consciousness, lie unawakened potentialities which, if brought into play, would better accomplish our daily tasks for us and spring to our assistance in moments of crisis and exceptional strain.

The times we live in do not help our predicament. Friction wears us out, and superfluous effort defeats its own ends. As a result, muscles respond clumsily, and decisions falter. Why experiment blindly with modern automation when, with understanding, the mere touch of a button releases such astounding power.

This is a period of mounting tensions. Never has there been such a need to preserve energy through serenity as in this atomic age.

Many of us are aware of what the world is doing to us and recognize our own reactions and their relation to our physiology, mental poise, and general well-being. Yet few of us make any effective effort to counterbalance the daily pressures.

It is a curious fact that, while we are always inventing and perfecting gadgets and striving for greater mechanical efficiency hardly one of us knows how to expend himself to the utmost, or is aware of how imperfectly we use our minds and bodies. We are more apt to devote time mastering the mechanism of a new device—with its essentially limited existence—than in exploring the possibilities of the human body, which is ours to use at will and which must last us a lifetime.

Body dynamics was designed to fill the present pressing need.

My method combines modern science and ancient wisdom. It unites a series of scientifically simple exercises with harmonious breath control and a certain intuitive way of looking at life.

It not only promotes muscular flexibility, but releases untapped sources of energy from deep within us and restores those natural forces of which we rob ourselves daily. City living and material preoccupations cut us off from nature and prevent our moving and acting naturally. Even sleep is becoming a lost art and all too frequently is artificially induced.

Body dynamics helps recapture precious birthrights.

It is a constant reminder that body and mind form one mysterious complex whole, that union of physical and mental efforts heighten perception and provide emotional gratification, as well as health and relaxation.

These are my aims:

1. To get better acquainted with our basic structure.
2. To take full advantage of its invaluable self-correcting equipment.
3. To experience joy in this!

You will find in these aims the excitement of vital discovery. As you follow the different routines, new avenues of accomplishment open before you. Your personality takes on greater assurance, with a body immediately responsive to your will and functioning to its utmost. This is a source of satisfaction which few outside pleasures give. You become a new person with a new point of view.

How is this brought about?

By creating a stronghold in regions of habitual weakness.

These regions, I have found, are the spinal column—particularly the lower back—the inner thighs and the abdominal wall. When these areas are strengthened and co-ordination of correct breathing with movement becomes automatic, the weight of the torso lifts itself off the hips, the head rests lightly on the spine, and the whole body feels air-borne. When air is pumped into a tire, it becomes expanded and buoyant. Naturally the tire has no consciousness of being expanded and buoyant. Nevertheless, it is. Similarly, when those areas of the body necessary to good body function are strengthened and correct breathing becomes habit—good posture automatically establishes itself.

Your new zest springs from a well-controlled center of body balance, whereby movement is liberated from inhibiting strictures, and you begin to assume naturally and unconsciously, the position which is best for everything you do—sleeping, walking, standing, sitting, reclining, dancing, and sports. This builds up endurance, multiplies energy, minimizes fatigue, and improves appearance.

In contrast to athletic systems or violent sports—many of which can be undertaken only by the relatively youthful—my exercises can be done by everyone. You do not have to be strenuous to keep in toned condition.

Actually, the aging process has less to do with the loss of agility and muscular elasticity than our indifference to, and neglect of the body's exact needs. Debutantes and grandmothers, little children and mature men can all get similar results. It is not necessary to go through time-consuming involved routines. With gentle persistence in a few crucially-important small movements, you draw upon a vitalizing flow of involuntary muscle play which automatically corrects, strengthens and restores. Your body works *for* you instead of *against* you. This makes all the difference in the world to the way it performs. Your body exults in the execution of movement conforming to its natural aptitudes.

Mechanized life has deprived us of many of the simple tasks that once afforded joy and fulfillment. It destroys our instinctual action, and we are the poorer for it. Restoring to the body its normal activities and giving it things to do which bring its various parts into spontaneous response are of fundamental importance. It lifts the curtain which has come down between mind and body, fosters harmony between inward and outward concerns, and imparts a radiance to living.

Most doctors admit the enormous influence that thinking and feeling have upon our physical condition. We can, if we will, actively affect the state of our health for good or ill. This is a demonstrable truth which becomes self-evident in my working sessions.

Here I encourage participation in forces greater than ourselves; here we strive to become actually all that we potentially are. My routines express the interdependence of spirit and matter. In a continuous folding and unfolding of the body, in a beautifully co-ordinated flow of motion, we truly feel what is meant by moving in harmony with the universal rhythm. We live out the equivalent of world pulses, and experience with increasing awareness, the *positive* and *negative* charges of the body. And in time, we come to equate these with the positive and negative aspects of everything about us—the good and bad in life, the heights and depths of our own nature.

My exercises establish a more meaningful correspondence between everyday life and our own particular conflicts. In serving the body they tend to widen horizons and to raise our sights. They not only relieve aches and pains, but help resolve the tension of opposing forces always battling within us—our alternating pettiness and real self-sacrifice, our devouring fears and the courage to surmount them, our agonizing struggles with conscience—all these find satisfying expression in my Body Dynamics.

The following is the core of my work.

My system has an affinity with oriental teaching. It releases the unconscious and makes the resultant energy available for daily living. It comprises activity which includes inactivity, and inactivity which is activity, in a continuous flowing circle.

The establishing of good body balance is combined with rhythmical breathing. The relation of the latter to unhampered movement is little understood outside the Orient. There, it is recognized as the mainspring, not only of physical, but of spiritual power. Its application to Body Dynamics helps differentiate my work from mechanical gymnastics, or the traditional routine of the army drill sergeant intent only on muscular strength.

Yet my approach to this subject is entirely practical. The student does not spell it out in so many words. My work is dramatic, not dogmatic. No one stops to philosophize. Conscious thought can interfere with motion, and with too much deliberation, the valuable unconscious is lost.

The student comes to understand my method by immediate experience. From the very first lesson he gains a new concept and is encouraged by the ease with which movement follows movement in orderly progression, until the most difficult seems simple. All awareness of self vanishes and a serene self-forgetfulness sets in. Time and again, my students have experienced this blissful condition and have come to realize that the ego often blocks the way to understanding and enlightenment.

By getting out of our own way and surrendering to an unself-conscious attitude, we end by deepening our comprehension. This is one of those eternal paradoxes, like losing one's life to preserve it, or any other of the great truths which we readily accept but which, from time to time, must be re-examined and restated.

Self-detachment, *learning to let go,* is the most necessary step toward surpassing mere technical competence in physical work. The physical goal is an effortless ease comparable to that of some beautiful forest animal or of the cat, which owes its grace to its perfect command of relaxation.

Breath control throughout all the exercises is important, but it does not play an occult role. Body Dynamics does not impinge on Yoga practice, in which mastery of breathing becomes a prime spiritual objective. This ritualistic concept is readily accepted in the Orient where such great emphasis is placed upon breathing that whole schools of philosophy have been founded on the 'Science of Breath'. Body Dynamics is similar to, and draws inspiration from Zen Buddhism, in which the practical quest for self-knowledge and development seems, above all other oriental teachings, most acceptable to the American pragmatic temperament.

Zen is neither religion nor philosophy; it is a *way of life*. It deals not only with abstruse ideas. It is so vital and elusive that it escapes definition; it is not so much understood as lived. Zen teaches that too elaborate preparation of the mind creates inner tensions that curtail spontaneity. Zen masters insist that enlightenment—salvation—call it what you will— can be found in everyday things, that there is no division between the *ordinary* and the *extraordinary* in life. We grasp these truths and seize their significance in a sudden flash of recognition, which the Zen sect calls satori. This can happen at the sight of some common occurrence: the fall of a rock, a lovely flower, or the contemplation of a sunset. For reality is not only something outside ourselves—it is also within us. We have only to look.

I came to many of these conclusions, independently. In working out a new approach to physical education, I felt that I must make it part of a wider conception of human experience. And I found in Zen Buddhism much to confirm my own theories.

The search for balance and a new center of gravity, the functioning in unison of the mental and physical, the emancipation of self for the purpose of making the body an instrument of spiritual development; all this I learned, has its counterpart in many aspects of this oriental training. Even its seeming casualness is echoed in my own avoidance of theoretical discussion in class. However do not be misled by such simplicity.

My basic exercises included in this book are those which can be done easily without the help of a teacher. My work, however, goes to the heart of things. It touches mainsprings not only of health, but of reality and life.

2 Rest Assured

The Art of Relaxation

It may seem odd that a book on Body Dynamics should begin with a chapter on sleep. The relationship is not hard to find. Sleep is a source of energy. Your body in repose is the same bony structure which must be kept upright all day. The relaxed muscles holding the nightly position are the same which bring you into daily action.

The way you lie in bed influences the way you stand and walk.

You spend about a third of your life on a mattress. Most of us do not sleep all that time. We are too tense, too emotionally worn to unwind and give ourselves the rest we need. Unable to relax, we toss and turn, adding irritation to fatigue. Sleeping pills and all the tranquilizing aids, which are rapidly becoming a major national industry, do not always bring relief.

Sleep finally claims us and what happens then? Almost invariably we slump into the attitude mankind has inherited since time began. The spine curves into a prenatal huddle. The head droops forward and down; the knees creep upwards to meet it. The arms fold over the torso. This is the protective wary posture of most animals.

It was the posture of primitive man when he came out of the cave. Shrinking into itself as though for warmth, the body was, nevertheless, ready for instant action in case of attack. It was correctly poised to roll over and fight, or run off—on all fours. But what was necessary for humans in those days, is no longer suitable to man under modern conditions. That huddle is an actual deterrent to his present stance. He still is not completely adapted to walking upright with ease.

For literally hundreds of centuries the strenuous conditions of primeval existence counteracted the effects of man's sleeping position. Men hunted and fought for food and hewed trees for fire and shelter. Women tilled and sowed, drew water from wells, and carried heavy burdens. Life provided its own remedy.

Today we put up the thermostat when we are cold. Much of our food comes packaged and prepared. Modern gadgetry spares us work but takes its human toll as well.

For all its wonderful conveniences, our world, apparently, weighs more heavily upon us than it did on our Neanderthal ancestors. Even though we have walked erect for so long, we still slump at night, and modern existence provides no natural correctives; we wake up mornings wondering why we are tired, why our hands tingle with "pins and needles," why we are full of so many aches and pains.

Few connect this with the way we lie in bed. The truth is, most of us do not know how to sleep.

We have not acquired the ability to stretch out relaxed,

completely surrendering to the great healer, sleep. Taut nerves and muscles show we are not at peace with ourselves. There is not enough core of unity within us to resist the pressures and fragmentation of modern living.

Men and women take their problems to bed with them, It is a rare individual who banishes—let alone solves—nagging thoughts. No one is completely free from this torment, for no one can evade worrying obligations and conflicts. These are a part of life itself.

Only the oriental sage or the exceptional artist can withdraw into ideal detachment. Most of us are tied to a pattern of behavior established by a hundred trivial details. This pattern can be altered. If we want serenity we must achieve it within our present environment, not by attempting to escape. Once we achieve it, we must maintain an even balance no matter what outside forces tug at our being; we must remain whole and strong in the midst of constant interruptions and demands.

All this is possible, as you will presently see. To begin with, you must rediscover the blessing of natural sleep.

Synonymous with life itself is the habit of breathing. Even in sleep, we never cease to breathe. We can do without food and even without water for short periods. But without air there is no survival. Stop breathing, and death claims us within minutes.

By filling our lungs, and nourishing our blood, air builds up a potent life-source. Every human activity depends upon the precious stuff. Without oxygen, food would do us no good, for it could not be oxidized and transmuted into healthy blood cells and body tissue. We simply *must* be oxygenized.

"But where can I obtain this oxygen?" asked one of my eager pupils, evidently determined to go right out and order a big supply of the wonder-working element. Indeed, if it were really an expensive item in our budget, we would probably all strain our resources to the limit to buy plenty of it.

Machines burn fuel to produce power. We must burn the body fuel in our cells to produce the same combustion or explosive energy. Deep breathing drives the carbon dioxide out of the blood stream and rejuvenates our whole system by circulating fuel to cells and organs.

The importance of correct breathing is recognized by all the great teachers. The Book of Genesis speaks of the mysterious energy, the Spirit (breath) of Life which animates the life process. Oriental masters consider it the source of spiritual strength, prime mover of its abundant flow. Some Yoga adepts build a system of meditation around psychic exercises in inhaling and exhaling air. With practice and intense application they can perform seeming miracles, such as sending themselves into a trance and suspending normal functioning.

Body Dynamics does not follow such techniques. It needs neither esoteric behavior nor abstract thoughts. It applies exercise strictly to daily needs; and correct breathing to revitalize our starving blood cells is definitely one of these.

FIG. 1

The following exercises are for all who would sleep well, and particularly for those to whom sleep comes with difficulty.

Lie on your back on retiring, the legs extended, arms at the sides, the palms turned down. (Fig. 1)

Make it a habit to take a few easy breaths. Inhale through the nostrils; exhale gently through the mouth. Note that relaxation is accomplished merely by continuous deep exhalation.

Inhale through the nostrils, and exhale slowly, opening the mouth wide as though you are yawning. Repeat 3 or 4 times. Yawning relaxes the muscles of the heart and the solar plexus.

Now, as you inhale, slowly raise the extended arms slightly, exhaling as the arms sink back at your sides. The arms should rise and sink slowly and rhythmically, the

33

wrists completely relaxed. (Fig. 2) This ebb and flow movement is like the ebb and flow of waves; as the arms rise, the hands droop limply downwards; as the arms sink, the hands waft gently backwards. (Fig. 2A)

Repeat this movement, this time raising the arms a little higher to shoulder level. Breathe in, as the arms rise; breathe out, as the arms slowly sink.

This flexible play of wrist and hand is included whenever the arms are used in co-ordinating breathing with movement. It is basic in Body Dynamics.

As you continue this gentle breathing it begins to assume a beautiful rhythm of its own. It is soothing as the gentle roll of waves on the shore and as reassuring as the steady heartbeat which throbbed about us long before we were born. Within ten minutes you are no longer conscious of doing an exercise, and the action becomes effortless. Rather than breathing, you feel that you are "being breathed."

"It" has taken over from our busy minds. Deep breathing has become automatic.

At this point it is easy to understand how a Yoga follower can go into a kind of trance-like ecstacy. We, too, find that deep rhythmic breathing can bring a wonderful detachment. We reach a state of mind in which nothing is planned or directed. Our thoughts are fixed on no particular place or thing. A melting drowsiness overcomes us, bringing peace.

Like a pool which brims over when it is replenished, we, too, experience a satisfying sense of outpouring. But we are not drained and empty. We are refilled with inner harmony. This is a primordial sensation, open to everything, yet empty and free from attachments. Its symbol is the empty circle— the ancient Chinese cryptograph signifying much—for the circle is full of meaning to those who seek truth. Here again we are approaching the spirit of Zen, but not in order to

34

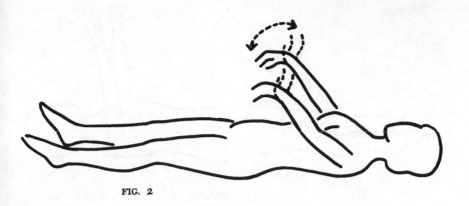

FIG. 2

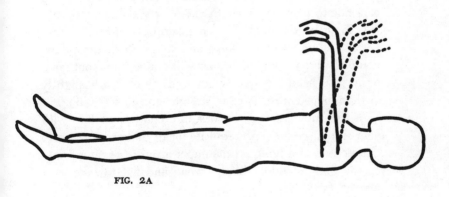

FIG. 2A

meditate or philosophize. That can induce tensions. It is enough for the moment that we have breathed ourselves into quiet self-forgetfulness.

Now you are ready for the correct position for sleeping.

35

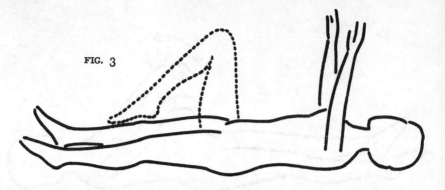

FIG. 3

With the last deep inhalation, draw up the right knee, and at the same time raise the arms to shoulder level. (Fig. 3) Roll over bodily to the left side as you gradually exhale with the arms descending. The left leg lies relaxed and the right crosses it comfortably; the arms lie limply across the body. (Fig. 4)

Now bank a small pillow under your head only, taking care not to place it under the neck or shoulders; the pillow may be doubled for more support and to ensure better alignment of the head and spine. With the pillow doubled under your head, you will notice how spontaneously your head tilts backwards, and the chin lifts slightly as though you were looking straight ahead. (Fig. 5)

At this moment your head is in a continuous line with your spine, the ideal prerequisite for its daily task. Be sure that you are not lying on the upper arm but resting firmly on the bony shoulder blade, broad and flat to take your weight. (Fig. 5A)

Do not be concerned if your body does not accept immediately this new way of sleeping; a little patience may be required to establish this position as second nature.

Do not be too demanding of yourself at first by trying to maintain it rigidly. Make whatever small adjustment of arms and legs necessary to individual comfort, and with gentle persuasion, you will find yourself unconsciously falling into

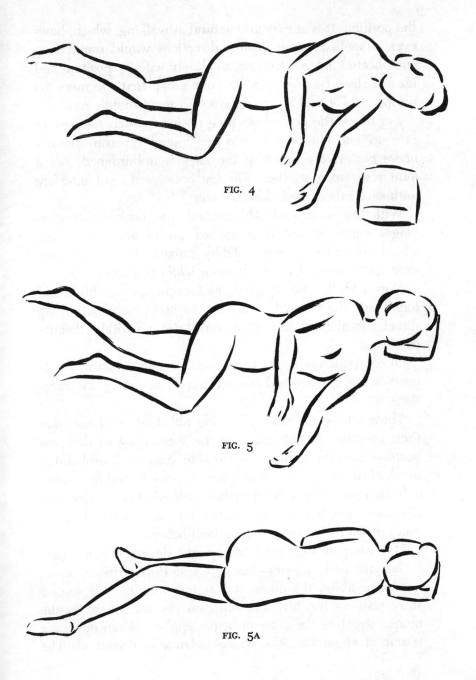

FIG. 4

FIG. 5

FIG. 5A

the position. It is as easy and natural as walking, which, however, if spelled out in explicit directions would sound very complicated indeed. In time, so closely will my position and idea of sleep be associated in your mind, that the mere assumption of it will be conducive to a good night's rest.

For this is the perfect sleeping position which releases all pressure and tension. There is not a single pressure on any nerve center. The small of the back is unburdened; not a joint rests upon another. The leg muscles do not interfere with each other; the ankles are free.

With the head perfectly aligned, the neck muscles no longer sag or strain. It is not advancing age, remember, which brings those crepey flabby throats. These can come from faulty muscular activity *even while you sleep.*

Now, with the chin uplifted, the face muscles are lifted and toned, and the throat is swanlike. All night long that strong direct line of head and spine constitutes a veritable beauty treatment.

Of course, if you prefer to rest on the right side, this whole position can be switched around, merely reversing the directions.

Those who complain of "moving all night" will find that their constant shifting may now be a changing of this new position from the right to the left side. And in all probability much of the restlessness will cease. Tossing in bed is so often a futile search for a comfortable, relaxed way of sleeping. My recommended position evades all the usual bad habits that impose such a strain on our well-being.

Man has paid dearly for his upright stance. It is not easy to balance body masses—the legs and thighs, trunk, arms, head—one above the other. Just as in a building the second story rests on the first, the third on the second, so in the human structure the same principle applies. When one mass is out of alignment, the whole balance is disturbed. The slightest deviation can do this. So great is the co-ordination between all parts of the body that when one is out of kilter all parts suffer. A sort of architectural disorder prevails, and we begin to feel pain or discomfort, usually in the lumbar spine regions.

Lower backache is one of the most common ailments in America. It spares neither man, woman, or child. Although this is sometimes caused by other problems, in nine cases out of ten, it can be traced to poor distribution of weight. We suffer from the effort of walking and sitting erect, which after all the eons we have been at it, we still do imperfectly. Bad posture is the curse of modern life, the greatest thief of good health.

A basic preparation for tackling this vital problem is *sleeping in the right position*. This means:

Not lying with the face buried on the arm (which alters circulation and causes numbness) but with the body balanced sideways, supported on the bony shoulder structure,

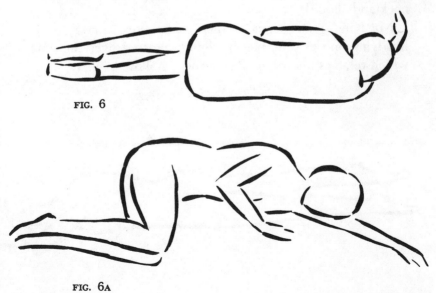

FIG. 6

FIG. 6A

FIG. 7

thus permitting the arms to hang down, free and relaxed at the sides.

Not using a high pillow which thrusts the head and neck forward (creating strain and tension of neck and shoulder muscles, the chief cause of the head-poking stance) but with head banked and aligned with the spine, thus releasing all neck and shoulder tension.

Not lying on the back (which contributes to sway-back) but lying on the side, one leg lightly crossed over the other which relieves and corrects a sway or hollow back.

FIG. 8

Not sleeping with the arms high over the head (which retards circulation and can result in unpleasant tingling in the hands) but with the arms hanging limply, thus aiding circulation and reducing demands on the heart.

Figures 6, 6A, 7, 8 and 9 illustrate some of the many incorrect sleeping postures.

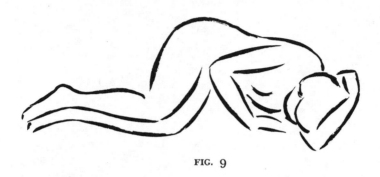

FIG. 9

In the position I have worked out, you will find deep satisfaction and real rest, as all parts of the body are comfortable. Pregnant women have told me that this posture has been their salvation. Martyrs to backache find in it positive relief from their pain. Nervous sleepers who clench their jaws and grind their teeth, do neither, as long as they are in this position. Their teeth part slightly, like a child's with the tip of the tongue gently touching the upper row; the lips remain closed.

With a little practice and perseverance, the sleeping position recommended becomes second nature. It is the body's signal for sleep. You will fall into it spontaneously, oblivious to everything, and drift off dreamily as on a cloud.

The next morning, after a night of complete relaxation, and with the lower spine strengthened, the skeletal structure is ready to support you upright without effort or strain. You start the day with zest.

FIG. 10   CORRECT SLEEPING POSITION

FIG. 10A   CORRECT SLEEPING POSITION

3 Building Beauty and Posture

on the Floor

Good posture is one form of beauty every woman can attain. It is hers at no cost and with very little effort. It will make her outstanding among other women and contribute more to the vitally important first impression she makes than anything her face and figure can convey.

No one can alter features or height; cosmetics and attractive hair-styling will transform only to a certain degree. But the plainest woman can walk like a queen. She can acquire an erect elegant carriage and swing along with a youthful elastic step even when youth has long since fled.

A beautiful posture dominates the personality. It is even more expressive than tone of voice or the most fashionable and expensive clothes. It is the secret of that aura of agelessness which envelops some women (and men too) and which,

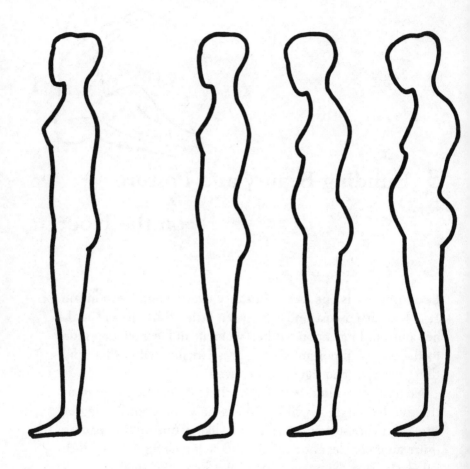

FIG. 11

as the years creep on, becomes an increasingly desirable asset.

Good posture has advantages far beyond mere appearance for men as well as women. Just as a weak body is a handicap everywhere in life, so a strong well-poised one promotes health and physical well-being (both of which, in turn, help build a fine posture).

Most of the vital organs responsible for our well-being are situated in the abdominal cavity, supported and surrounded by a great sheath of muscle. Immediately above them is the chest cavity, containing the heart and the lungs, separated from the abdomen by the diaphragm, another muscular sheath partitioning the trunk practically at the middle. It is precisely at this middle point that middle age sets in. Once this muscular structure becomes toneless and flabby, suppleness vanishes, the torso thickens, and it is good-bye forever to youthful looks, unless you do something about it.

And believe me, there is plenty you can do!

The spinal column, as you know, is such a delicately complicated mechanism that the slightest deviation from the normal position places a strain on muscles and nerves. This, in time, produces aches and pains and is a contributing factor to nervous tension.

The pelvic bones at the base of the spine are immediately affected by any spinal maladjustment. Capable of little action themselves, they tend, under unfavorable conditions, to tip forward dragging down the internal organs and increasing the muscular strain in this area. The inevitable result is to accentuate the curve of the lower back, causing much distress and fatigue. (Fig. 11)

The big thigh bone (the femur) joins the pelvic basin in a ball-and-socket joint, ready for action in all directions. Most of us do no more than move it forward and back. Consequently, the muscles on the outside of the thigh get very little exercise, and the inner thigh muscles get practically none. Although these muscles respond to activation more quickly than any others, an unsightly bulge usually occurs here. That middle-aged "settled" look is due to soft pads of fat on the thighs. The telltale "spread" behind you comes from long-sitting on the rear hip muscles, with the buttocks protruding and, quite frequently, one hip thrown out in the odd angular pose inspired by (or inspiring!) modern painters.

Watch a group of women climb a flight of stairs. Their pathetic waddle reveals just how incorrectly all these muscles are used. As for the abiding beauty of the long gently curved thigh which could be every woman's pride, it is found only in youthful bathing beauties and the eloquence of poets!

Last, but not least in the category of bone and muscle holding us upright, are those Cinderellas of all body parts— our delicate, intricate, mistreated feet. How we abuse these precious possessions! And how terribly they take their revenge!

Neglected, tortured feet put more premature lines into the face than all the ravages of advancing years. Distress spreads to every part of the body. Headache, backache, ragged nerves, poor circulation, and indigestion are often traceable to bad feet. This marvelous conglomeration of exquisite bones and tendons must not only support the whole body, but must be sufficiently resilient to propel the weight forward in walking and to absorb all shocks. Here again we face the same terrible dilemma. Poor foot work produces bad posture, and bad posture reacts disastrously on the feet, causing fallen arches and tightened tendons which in turn affect the legs and upper thighs.

When you consider that a single toe movement brings about twenty different muscles into play, the importance of

48

the feet in standing erect and walking beautifully cannot be exaggerated.

All in all, there is a high degree of instability in the composition and employment of our bodies. They are so delicately sensitive to small disturbances and maladjustments that their persistence in functioning over decades of bad treatment seems little short of miraculous.

Fortunately, they respond to incredibly minute stimulations. Much of their mechanism could be likened to the movement of a watch spring, which slight in itself, nevertheless maintains a steady tick of infinite significance. When the clock is wound, it quietly ticks itself away. When we are wound, our tensions accumulate, and we must learn how to unwind them. Fortunately, we are provided with certain self-regulatory arrangements which we can bring into play. *This* is our good fortune!

Few of us are willing to devote much time to exercise. The very word has become distasteful, with its implication of muscular exertion and physical discomfort. It bores us and seems to have so little practical application. Who wants to lift weights or run marathons? Most regular setting-up systems have been handed down from old-fashioned Swedish or German army drill routines and have little relation to the natural movements of everyday life. This kind of physical education is radically wrong because its chief objective is to develop the physical faculties without bringing them any closer to our inner consciousness. We are taught gymnastics, calisthenics, or whatever you may call it. We learn to swim, jump, run, and play strenuous games. And still, after many years of these activities, we cannot deal with the simplest problems of good posture, in sitting, standing, or walking. We hurry through our daily dozen as indifferently and uninspiredly as in the old weekly gym class and then slump right back into our old slouch.

If it were only possible to relate physical education to some inner satisfaction, find fulfillment for ourselves as well as uninhibited movement, gratify that urge to escape from prisons of our own making, and exult in the drive and force of creative energy!

You can if you will.

Body Dynamics makes such possibilities become realities. It brings vibrant health and regenerates energy centers. You may think it is just recreation and find it is, in truth, a re-creation.

Fantastic, you say?

Not any more fantastic than the world around us.

For how many centuries did pitchblende appear inert until radium was discovered in it? That which had always been static was suddenly revealed to be perpetually in motion. Seemingly solid mineral was crammed with dynamic energy. It had always been there, but someone had to find it. In Body Dynamics you find your own radium, your own dynamic self.

To begin, you lie down on the floor.

It is better that the spine become accustomed to a hard wooden surface. On a soft mat or mattress, it is liable to accommodate itself and defeat our efforts for good alignment. In these exercises the chief objectives are to strengthen and straighten the spine by correcting the weakened area created by the exaggerated arch, a condition commonly known as sway- or hollow-back.

Let the arms and legs extend in a comfortable, relaxed position with the eyes closed. The body feels heavy, slack, and detached from everything. You have no thought or sensation other than lying there outstretched, surrendering every part of yourself to gravity.

Feel that you are a little rowboat tethered to a country pier, with lazy waves lapping at the sides till they gently unloose the knot which holds you to the post. You are utterly at ease as you go drifting off through empty space towards the horizon. The head rolls rhythmically—carried by its own weight from side-to-side, without strain in the chin, neck, or shoulders. You discover how a simple movement that satisfies can bring about a highly beneficial result. You become free of the restless pressures of your everyday mind.

Now gently draw up the right foot and place it on the floor near the seat. Gently place the left in a similar position, soles flat and heels together. Your arms are at your sides, palms turned down. (Fig. 12) (We bring up the feet one at a time to conserve the energy of bringing them up together.)

A good thing to realize at the very beginning is, that at no time while executing any of the movements should the shoulders rise and fall in breathing. The neck and shoulder muscles, usually overanxious to participate, should always be relaxed, unless the movement specifically demands their participation.

FIG. 12

Visualize the classic beauty of the human form as represented in sculpture. Whether in positions of repose or action, the shoulders are down, expressively quiet.

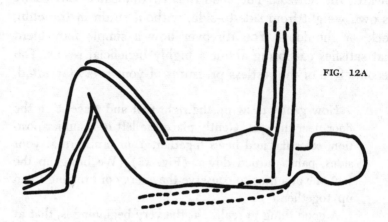

FIG. 12A

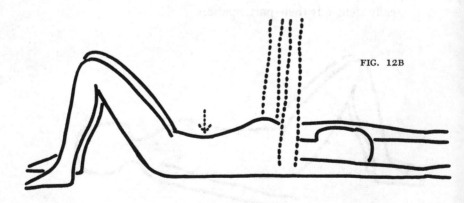

FIG. 12B

Slowly take a deep breath, lifting the arms slightly; exhale while they return to the floor at your sides. Increase your inhalation as the arms rise higher. Repeat this several times and as you breathe out, try to imagine the air escaping from the small of your back. Picture the back of a rubber baby doll where the air comes out for the squeak. Imagine *that* is where you are breathing out. Breathe out firmly, and as you do so, you will feel the spine relax and settle comfortably flush with the floor.

As you continue to breathe in through the nostrils, bring the arms to a standing position (Fig. 12A); and as you exhale "through the small of the back" allow the arms to flow back overhead to rest on the floor.

Inhale as you raise the arms *only* to the standing position—exhale as you lower them overhead to the floor. Continue this rhythmical breathing, while raising and lowering the arms, until it becomes natural to you. The abdominal wall draws itself in without any effort; the action of breathing out purposefully and completely produces this effect. (Fig. 12B)

You can check the steady outward flow of air by softly humming, as the air escapes. When the last note dies away and your arms are overhead, take a full breath, and with one sweeping exhalation, let the arms flow forward down to your sides. Inhale as the arms sweep back overhead. Continue doing this a few times.

You are beginning a liberating breath control with new and far-reaching consequences. As oxygenation increases, the body tissues are flooded—the whole system is flushed with a God-given source of elation.

Have both feet flat on the floor when you start. Take a deep breath. Exhale, as you raise the left foot, gently lifting the knee towards the chest. Inhale as you replace that foot on the floor. Then exhale as you draw up the other foot, while that knee moves towards the chest. (Fig. 13)

Continue this movement three or four times in an easy "walking rhythm"; co-ordinate your breathing with it. Remember that one foot is always flat on the floor when the other is raised; that you always exhale, gently but fully, as the knee moves toward the chest. This very familiar action, relieved of all the weight involved in real walking, is curiously soothing. It disperses any tension which may build up with beginners; it forms a good prelude to exercise and a pleasant interlude during later work.

Co-ordination of breathing with movement should be the aim in the beginning, but must not be thought of as an end in itself. Correct breathing is a deliberate, conscious process, and it takes time to break up old habit patterns and establish new ones. So do not be overanxious at first. Once you are aware of this new way of integrating breathing with activity, it almost establishes itself, and becomes easy, unconscious and natural.

You are now going to begin a sequence of movements which has been proven most helpful in correcting and strengthening the spine, especially the area of the lower back.

Raise the left foot and place it flat on the right thigh. Let it remain there comfortably for a moment; then put it down on the floor again and raise the right foot, placing it on the left thigh. (Fig. 14)

Here again the breathing is the same as in the "walking movement." Inhale when you begin with both feet flat on the floor. Exhale as you place one foot on the thigh; *inhale* as the foot returns to the floor. Continue doing this a few times.

FIG. 13

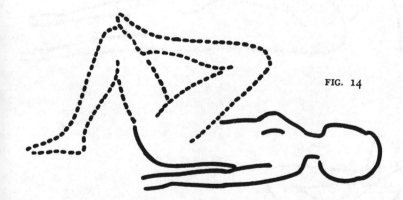

FIG. 14

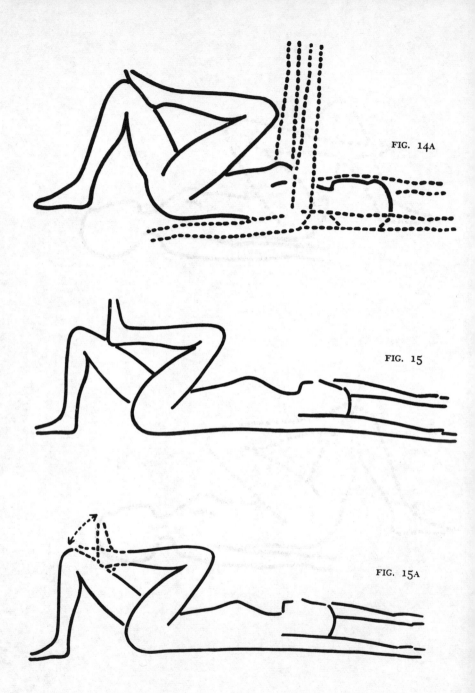

FIG. 14A

FIG. 15

FIG. 15A

Keep the left foot on the right thigh. Then breathe in deeply as you raise the arms to a vertical (standing) position, at right angles to the body and exhale slowly as they return to your sides on the floor. Repeat several times, remembering to inhale as the arms are raised, and exhale as they are lowered. Now change the foot position, by placing the right foot on the left thigh. Resume the arm movements and repeat a few times.

With the left foot on the right thigh, inhale as you bring your arms to shoulder level, exhale as they flow back to the floor overhead, inhale as they come up to shoulder level only, exhale as they return to the floor overhead. Continue rhythmically as you alternate the foot position. (Fig. 14A)

The flexible play of hands and wrists as the arms raise and lower is a gesture of infinite grace. The slow continuous repetition is like a flight of birds, or the steady rise and fall of waves. Its compelling rhythm fulfills a psychological need in you. Instinctively you are participating in a mysterious potent force. With that unbroken flow of motion you are moving in harmony with a world rhythm—the unending succession of day and night, of light and darkness, and of sunrise and sunset.

For further activity of the spine, extend the arms overhead on the floor and re-establish the simple "walking movement." Release by bringing the arms down at the sides and continue "walking."

Again place one foot on the other thigh. Raise and lower the foot by flexing the ankle in a rhythmic up-and-down movement (keeping the heel firm). This movement is done first with the arms at the sides, then with the arms overhead, resting on the floor. (Fig. 15) This extremely simple action demonstrates that you have a built-in apparatus for correcting your worst posture faults. This movement both secures the spine in a straight line flush to the floor and flattens the abdomen at the same time. The foot acts as a lever. (Fig. 15A) While the ankle is being exerted gently and all the foot muscles brought into action, this up-and-down movement coaxes the spinal column into its most healthful posture by sending impulses from vertebra to vertebra.

Sufferers from chronic backache and weakness often find immediate relief in this one exercise. How good it feels when the entire length of the spine is extended, relaxed, ironed out and secure. Besides the cessation of lower-back pain, you will find that these movements firm the inner thighs—areas of extreme inaccessibility and very difficult to tone. It would seem that no one has ever realized the efficacy of our own self-regulating mechanism. Instead of "struggling up the wall" (and anyone who has ever worked on a weak back knows what this means) in vain efforts to straighten and flatten the spine so as to eliminate sway-back, we practice a simple movement in utmost comfort and thus accomplish our objective. While doing this, *the body takes care of itself.*

Equal to the physical benefits you have already attained, is your heightened consciousness of the rhythm, the harmony, and the equilibrium inherent within you. With your center of balance established, you soon discover that it is the application of the "Law of Balance in Movement" *synchronized* with *proper breathing* that permits all future movements to be done with less expenditure of energy. The following exercises will show you how much easier they become as you continue.

Lie on the floor, with the feet together, soles flat on the floor, the arms extended at your sides, and palms down as in Fig. 12.

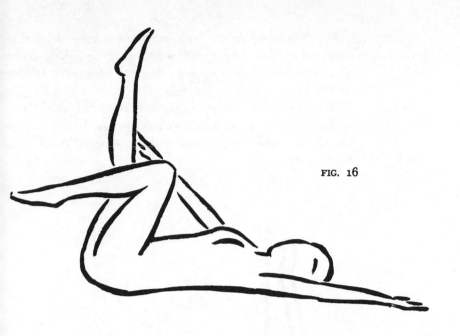

FIG. 16

Raise both arms back overhead to rest on the floor as you draw the right knee towards the chest.

The arms remain overhead as you draw the left knee towards the chest.

Now, with both knees towards the chest and both arms extended back overhead resting on the floor, take a full breath.

Exhale fully as you raise the right leg straight up, allowing the right arm to flow forward, hand to the leg. (Fig. 16)

Inhale as you flex the knees, and exhale as the arms flow back overhead to the floor. Be sure to take a full breath before you repeat the movement, several times with the right arm and leg, then with the left arm and leg; then alternate.

For Releasing: when both arms are overhead on the floor, take a full deep breath without strain; exhale completely as you sweep your arms down to your sides; inhale as you sweep them back overhead.

This is a good time to realize how rarely breathing for ordinary life purposes calls for complete exhalation. I have found that when exhalation is deep enough, inhalation takes care of itself.

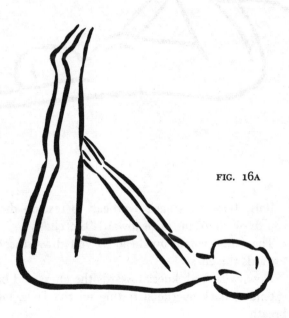

FIG. 16A

When you are ready, center yourself, anchor your spine, draw in the abdomen, release it, and then: Take a full easy breath, and as you exhale allow *both* legs to flow upwards as *both* hands extend towards the legs. (Fig. 16A) Inhale as you flex the knees and exhale as the arms

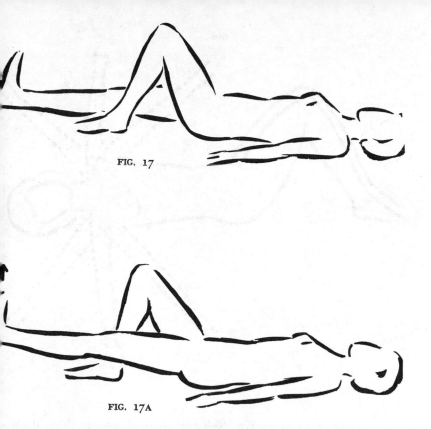

FIG. 17

FIG. 17A

flow back overhead to the floor. Repeat. You will become aware of how good it feels when the weight of the body is balanced on the solid base of the spine. The legs seem to flow out and up—to rise into space effortlessly.

With the feet on the floor close to the seat and arms comfortably at the sides, (1) extend the right leg to the floor with the foot drawn up from the ankle (2) return the leg to its original position and extend the left leg in the same way. (Fig. 17) Repeat a few times. (3) Continue the same movement, this time raising the leg about three or four inches above the floor as you extend it. (Fig. 17A) Notice how raising the leg as you extend it causes

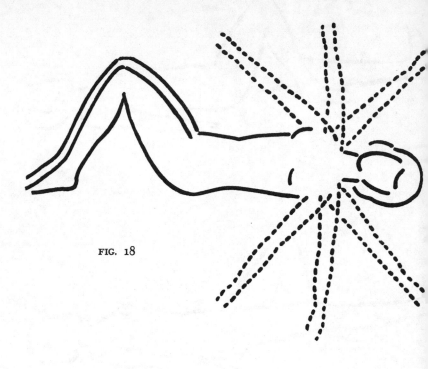

FIG. 18

the spine to anchor itself and the abdomen to draw itself in.

With the feet on the floor close to the seat, the arms extended a few inches away from your sides, and the palms up, roll the hips, slowly and gently from one side to the other, allowing the knees to roll in the direction of the floor.

As the hip swaying continues, the knees drop closer and closer to the floor and the arms glide higher gradually until they reach shoulder level and finally arrive outstretched overhead in V position. (Fig. 18) This swaying motion of the hips, combined with the arms in varying upward positions, brings the whole torso's muscular sheath into gentle action, stretching and relaxing it. As you raise the arms, each succeeding position brings different back-muscle groups into play. The exciting thing is the realization that *without any conscious stretching* on your part, the whole body is being subtly drawn out, and *it is doing its own stretching.*

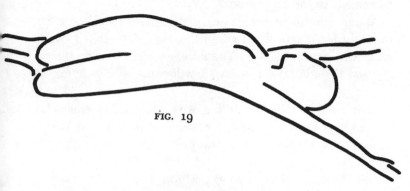

FIG. 19

Increase the momentum of this rolling or swaying movement till the knees touch the floor, first on one side and then on the other. Breathe easily and unhurriedly. Do not strain or exert yourself if your knees do not reach the floor at first—they will with practice. (Fig. 19)

With the arms extended overhead on the floor, clasp your hands, the thumb and four fingers of the right hand holding the four fingers of the left hand. Gently sway the hips from side to side, allowing the knees to roll in the direction of the floor. (Fig. 19A) This gives a delightful feeling of being thoroughly stretched through the torso.

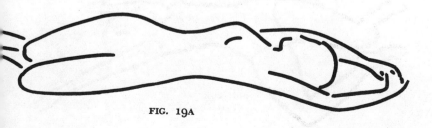

FIG. 19A

With the feet about 18 inches apart, soles flat on the floor, and the arms above the head in an open V position, roll the hips very slowly to the right side, the head rolling to the left. (Fig. 20) Return to center and be sure that the lower spine contacts the floor *before* you repeat the movement to the other side.

As the movement progresses, notice how the knee of the right leg practically fits into the arch of the left foot, and vice versa. (Fig. 20A) You may not be able to do this the first time, but don't worry—it will come with practice.

Now combine the hip rolling with an arm movement. As the hips fall to the left, carry the right arm over the body to the left side so that the palms touch each other. (Fig. 21)

Roll back to the starting position (both arms outstretched overhead) and continue the movement to the right side.

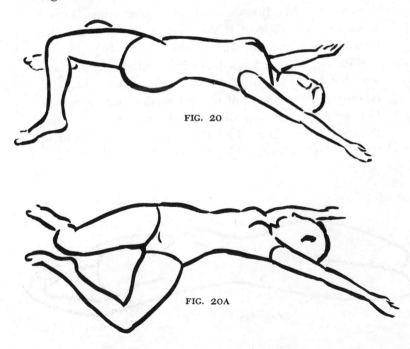

FIG. 20

FIG. 20A

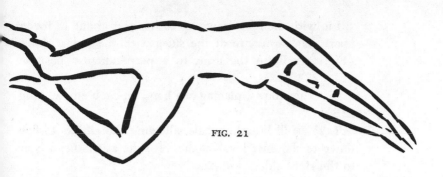

FIG. 21

Repeat from side to side. With this movement breathing is very easily co-ordinated. Take a full breath before you start. Exhale as the hips roll to the left side and the right arm is carried over the body. Inhale as the right arm flows back to the floor. Repeat on the other side. (Fig. 21A) Exhale as the hips roll to the right side and the left arm is carried over the body. Inhale as the left arm flows back to the floor—pause a moment—then exhale as both arms flow forward down to the floor at your sides. Continue with this co-ordinated rhythm. You have just experienced a complete cycle of rhythmic breath control.

FIG. 21A

Lie with the feet drawn up to the seat about 18 inches apart. The arms are at the sides with the palms down. (Fig. 22) Raise the arms to a perpendicular position. (Fig. 22A)

Flex the elbows, placing one hand on each elbow. (Fig. 22B)

Take a full breath; exhale, allowing the elbows to flow down to shoulder level, at the left side, as the head turns to the right side. (Fig. 22C)

Inhale as the arms return to center, and exhale as they flow to the other side. (Fig. 22D)

Return to center position. (Fig. 22B)

Take a full breath; exhale as the arms flow back overhead to rest on the floor. (Fig. 22E)

Inhale, bringing the arms up to standing. (Fig. 22B) Exhale as they return to the floor overhead. Repeat several times.

This conscious breathing in and breathing out of body and spirit will help you later to feel that you are walking on air—that you are moving elegantly as well as smoothly, at work or at play—that you are living beautifully and feeling exalted.

With the hands on the elbows, and arms overhead resting on the floor (Fig. 22E), close your eyes and try to recall the image of the simple "walking movement." Take all the time you need to think it through. Then do it. Next try to recall the image of extending the right leg to the floor with the foot drawn up from the ankle; remember that you return the leg to the original position before you extend the other one. See the completed movement several times. Then *do* it. Finally try to recall the image of the hips gently swaying the knees from side-to-side *before you do it.*

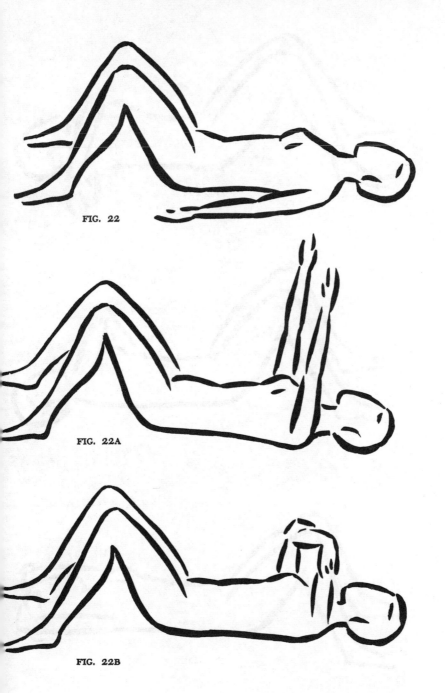

FIG. 22

FIG. 22A

FIG. 22B

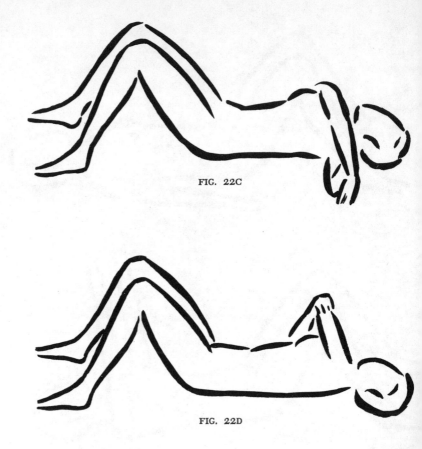

FIG. 22C

FIG. 22D

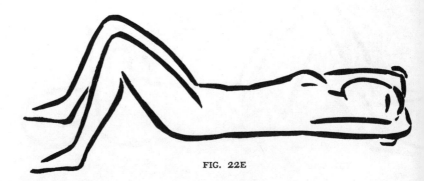

FIG. 22E

You will become aware of a mysterious source within you that not only relays messages to the senses, but increases the speed and precision of motor responses. You discover that these movement images actually help you to follow directions more readily, to do the movements with greater ease and sureness, and above all to deepen the experience of gaining conscious control of your body. Last but by no means least, this visualization of activity is a tremendous aid in relaxing the weary eye muscles.

The self-imposed restraint that you now experience in the area of the arms gives you some idea of how people live in the prisons of their own bodies without ever escaping. There is no greater joy than the joy of freedom after constraint. So, let your bells ring out! Let your arms fling wide open! Let your legs slide apart as they extend away on the floor! Let the joy of your complete release give you the fresh spirit of a pioneer—exploring the new world that has always been within you.

You are now ready for a series of movements that has been selected not only for beauty of sequence, but for the fundamental principles of movement in general and of balance in particular. Once this effortless way of moving has been acquired by practice, the everyday movements of life become complete exercises in themselves.

Lie on your back, with the spine well-anchored to the floor, feet close to the body, arms at the sides and the palms down.

FIG. 23

Draw the knees up (one at a time) towards the chest. Then place one hand on each knee with the arms fully extended.

Bring the knees towards the chest alternately—one arm is always fully extended as the other one flexes. (Fig. 23) This not only draws the shoulders down but eliminates activity of the ever-busy neck and shoulder muscles. Your head, shoulders and neck will become so relaxed you, too, will acquire a sculptured quality.

FIG. 23A

Continue the same movement, bringing *both* knees towards the chest and then extending *both* arms fully. Notice that it is deep elbow flexion that brings the knees towards the chest without straining either the neck or the shoulder muscles. (Fig. 23A) Notice also, how much more satisfying it is to inhale when the arms are extended and to exhale when the knees flow towards the chest. This movement sets up within you, a pleasant in-and-out rhythm, a coming and a going, and an ebb and flow.

With the arms fully extended and the hands on the knees, roll on your hips from one side to the other on the highest point of the hip muscle. (Fig. 23B) Turning your head to the opposite of the hip roll aids balance. Go to either side as far as you can maintain balance.

Now roll to the right side. Extend the upper leg (left) parallel to the floor, without any change in the position of the hand, which glides along on the thigh. (Fig. 23C) The extended leg returns to its original position and the knee flows back to the hand. Center yourself and feel how easily your spine rests on the floor. You roll over to the other side and extend the other leg (right) in the same way. Alternate a few times.

The emphasis on keeping the hand relaxed and its position unchanged as it glides along the thigh, is to eliminate the slightest possibility of wasted motion which not only means lost energy, but usually contributes to short, jerky, unattractive movements.

The next exercise is a continuation of the one above; only now as you extend your leg, let your arm flow back overhead close to the ear. (Fig. 23D) Alternate several times.

FIG. 23C

A further continuation of the exercise above: only now you add a leisurely unfoldment of both arms and both legs to their fullest capacity. Here again the movement is done

FIG. 23D

with greater ease by inhaling when the hands are on the knees and exhaling with the unfoldment of the arms and the legs. (Fig. 23E)

You will find that added to the power and fascination of these balanced, effortless movements is their sequential development. Each exercise is the natural extension of the one preceding it; each change of movement gently leads into the one to come. Imperceptibly you have developed automatic control in the performance of a series of movements which together form a beautiful, satisfying, rhythmic pattern. What

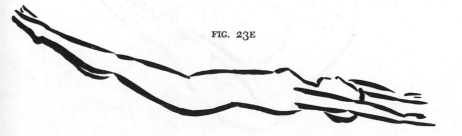

FIG. 23E

gives the greatest feeling of satisfaction is that *without consciously aiming* for it, the beauty of form and line and the grace of movement *establish themselves.*

What you are about to do next brings this entire series of movements to its ultimate expression.

> Lie on your back, with the knees towards the chest and the arms overhead resting on the floor. Notice how much stronger and well-anchored your spine feels now, as you center yourself.
>
> Take a full breath, then roll ever so slightly to one side. Exhale as you extend the arms and legs forward simultaneously. It is a complete and spontaneous unfoldment. (Fig. 24)
>
> The entire body in balance, on the highest point of the hip muscle, is a figure of extreme beauty; it looks as though it were air-borne. You feel weightless and exhilarated.

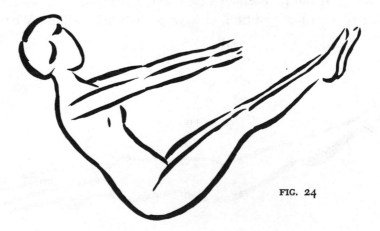

FIG. 24

FIG. 24A

The pose in Fig. 24B was chosen by one of France's greatest sculptors, Aristide Maillol, to symbolize flight. In a memorial to the war aviators of World War I, he created a figure which he calls *L'Air,* and a reproduction of this has just been presented to Yale University where it adorns the outdoor sculpture court. In spite of the heavy metal casting, this monu-

mental statue conveys the sensation of a floating figure and is considered the artist's masterpiece.

You, too, can attain a similar grace by practice and persistence. This air-borne attitude is well within your possibilities, once you become confident that your body is capable of such action. When you know *you can,* you venture to be all that *you are.*

One of my pupils came to me just five weeks after radical major surgery. She had made up her mind to regain her former mobility, grace and symmetry. With the encouragement of the class and her own courage reinforcing her self-knowledge, she re-educated her body and is now not only a star pupil, but assisting me as a teacher.

You have now completed your introductory set of exercises lying on the floor. Already you have accomplished a great deal. You have become better acquainted with your own mechanism, have learned to use it to your own advantage, and have begun to trust its power of accomplishment. Whatever doubts you may have had about its shortcomings have been dispelled by the realization that muscles respond almost gratefully, when coaxed into the action for which they were designed.

FIG. 24B (*opposite*) "L'AIR" BY ARISTIDE MAILLOL. *Courtesy of Yale University Art Gallery.*

Now, as you lie on the floor, take this opportunity to surrender completely to your essential needs.

This hour is yours, free from interruptions and clamorous demands; it is your time to gather your forces together; it is your time for the unification of your many selves. Every person should have a brief period of tranquility during the day; some time to be alone for contemplation, or a centering line of thought. This is indispensable if you are to maintain your strength for all the giving that life demands and to withstand the domestic, social, economic and community pressures that crowd you.

You are now gaining a better-functioning and better-looking body. Secure it with inner as well as outer growth. Make this session on the floor the time for replenishment. Even in a class, students reach their private havens, forget the presence of others, and carry back into everyday life their precious new-found serenity.

To accomplish this you must ignore, for a while, the dispersive daily activities and focus your attention on creative living. Focus on some purposeful assignment for yourself. You do not have to undertake a great project in order to salvage from your busy life a time for silence and solitude. Make your body your project; identify yourself with your aim.

Work with yourself. This makes you feel good and helps you to a greater understanding of your own personality. It leads, too, to a fuller understanding of others, for how can one comprehend others and treat them well, if one is heedless and neglectful of oneself?

With every body cell performing its appropriate function to the utmost, you are, spiritually as well as physically, better equipped for every future encounter. To do this is not to be self-centered. Your goal is to establish a stable center within you from which to reach out with greater confidence. You will have so much more to share when you have harvested this precious thing for yourself.

At the end of the longest practice session, far from feeling tired, you find yourself refreshed and ready for any task. For during the quiet period on the floor, you have been forming the valuable habit of thinking and feeling as a unit. *Action balancing emotion.* You could not have a better release of energy. You have been demonstrating the fundamental oneness of mind and body and finding in it an equilibrium and source of enrichment that sparks vitality. An incandescence glows in your face; all that is loftiest in you is finding an outlet. Even your friends will notice the difference in your spirit.

The husband of one of my pupils was only too willing to drive her to the weekly far-distant class "because she is so much happier and better-tempered when she goes," he confided to me.

A busy housewife confessed to me once, "If I don't go on with the lessons, my mean old self comes through."

This seems to show that both these pupils had acquired a new dimension, an added facet to their lives. They had found the way to a state that can only be described as "living in grace."

FIG. 25   CHINESE BODHISATTVA. *Courtesy of the Art Institute of Chicago.*

4 Sitting Pretty

The Zen Way

All of the usual daily activities, as well as most sports—golf, tennis, skiing, and even gardening—require particular elasticity in the lumbar region. It is from this area that our muscles must extend themselves and become limber and uninhibited so as to achieve moments of greater energy than those of work-a-day life. How often we suffer from strained muscles, or a pulled tendon when we spring into some unaccustomed position, making demands where demands are rarely made!

We will now begin exercises with the emphasis on greater forward flexion—exercises which will so influence your recreational and sports activities that they will even affect your golf score.

From our work on the floor we now go without breaking the continuity into a natural, comfortable, sitting posture. It

FIG. 25A

is a happy surprise to see how easily this is accomplished.

Lie on your back with the arms extended overhead, the knees towards the chest, and the ankles crossed.

Take a deep breath. Exhale fully as you roll up to a sitting position, tailor-fashion; place the hands on the knees and draw the spine erect. (Fig. 25A)

FIG. 25B

Place the palm of your right hand as far forward on the floor as you can without strain. Replace the hand on the knee, then extend the left hand in the same way.

As you continue this alternating movement, it sets up a gentle forward and backward rocking rhythm, coming from the lower back area.

83

Still sitting tailor-fashion, clasp the ankles with your hands, uncross the legs, and bring the soles of the feet together. (Fig. 26) Take a deep breath.

Exhaust the breath and flex the elbows while the body flows forward naturally. (Fig. 26A)

Inhale as you straighten the arms. Repeat. In this position, the seat centers itself squarely, establishes the aware-

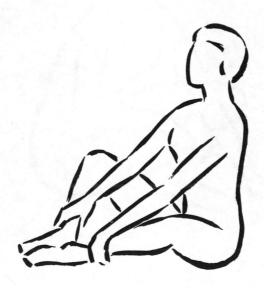

FIG. 26

ness of the "sitting bones"—an essential detail, to be remembered and utilized, especially by those who spend long hours on chairs.

Exhale deeply whenever the movement carries you forward. Think of blowing at an imaginary feather floating in front of you. That long sustained blowing while exhaling will automatically suck in the abdomen as it strengthens and releases tension in the lower back.

FIG. 26A

FIG. 26B

With the knees still drawn up and the hands clasping the ankles, place the feet comfortably apart, resting on their outer margins. (Fig. 26B)

Alternately release your hold on the ankles and pat the floor in front of your feet, first with the palm of one hand and then with the other.

Keep the head in line with the spine by raising the chin a little, as you continue this forward and backward movement, easily and rhythmically. For variation drop the head instead of raising the chin.

FIG. 26C

Now place the hands on the knees. Pat the floor in front of your feet, first with the palm of one hand and then with the other. (Fig. 26C and D)

It is interesting how this action, although almost identical with the former, brings into play other muscle groups. The purpose of these exercises is to become conscious of relaxing this lower back area. Always avoid any feeling of forcing. You will be surprised at how much is accomplished by exerting only the gentlest effort.

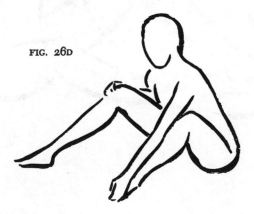

FIG. 26D

Sit with the knees drawn up and the feet apart, resting on their outer margins.

Breathe in deeply as you extend the arms forward, a little above shoulder level with the hands clasped.

Breathe out as your arms flow forwards down to the floor to your feet, and beyond if you can.

Drawing the arms in and up toward the chest, out and down towards the feet, sets up a rhythmical circular motion, and the breathing is co-ordinated naturally. (Fig. 27)

FIG. 27

FIG. 27A

It feels as if you were breathing your whole torso forward, and with the deeper expulsion of breath (which by now happens automatically) greater extension in the lower spine permits increased forward extension of the arms.

Extend the arms fully forward and down as far as is comfortable. Tap the floor with the hands (still clasped) a few times. (Fig. 27A) You will discover the origin of the spring-like action to be the base of the spine. This movement also has a releasing effect on the spine and lower back area.

Sit with the knees drawn up and the soles of the feet together. Clasp the ankles with the hands and do not release the hands until the entire movement is completed. (Fig. 28)

Slide one leg out, then bring it back to the original position (soles together). (Fig. 28A)

Slide the other leg in the same way.

Allow your head to flow with the movement as you extend from side to side.

This continuous alternating rhythm that slides the legs out and in—that brings play through the shoulders—that rocks the body forward and back—that stretches and releases the spine—gives the feeling that *not you* but your *built-in exerciser* has been set into action.

What fun to be merely going along for the ride!

Sit with legs outstretched as far apart as is comfortable. Raise the arms to shoulder level and clasp the hands.

Sway the hips in a circular movement towards the right; reverse the sway and circle toward the left.

This is a basic exercise, preparatory to further flexion of the pelvic area. Here again the shoulders merely "go along for the ride" as they benefit from this rotary movement.

The greatest gentleness should be exerted in all the sitting exercises, for their object is to strengthen the trunk and attain its greater forward movement with increased freedom in the lumbar region and inner thighs.

You will be surprised, at first, to discover how very little forward flexion you have. Do not feel discouraged. With coaxing and loving care, the muscles respond and begin to "give." Bodies are wonderfully co-operative if we are good to them and persuade them that we know their capacities and are willing to "*draw* them out."

FIG. 28

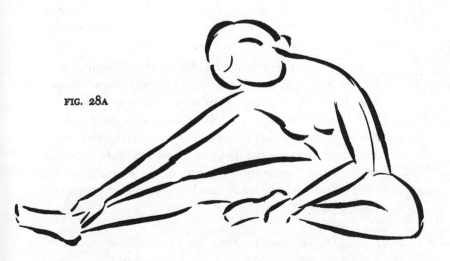

FIG. 28A

FIG. 29

Sit with the legs extended as far apart as is comfortable. Do not force the spread; the angle will increase with practice. Lean forward and clasp the ankles (the leg if you cannot reach the ankles). Inhale and then exhale, slightly flexing and extending the arms, as your body flows gently forward and backward. Deeper inhalation and exhalation, with greater flexion and extension of the arms, brings the body forward more easily and the hands closer to the ankles. (Fig. 29)

Now, as you lean forward, try to touch the toes of the right foot with the right hand; the left hand remains on or near the left ankle. (Fig. 29A) Replace the right hand on or near the right ankle and try to touch the toes of the left foot with the left hand. Alternate in this way several times.

Then bring both hands on or near the toes and slide the legs together, then wide apart. Repeat a few times. Practice this with patience. Even after a few minutes of these movements you begin to see how much more supple you are.

FIG. 29A

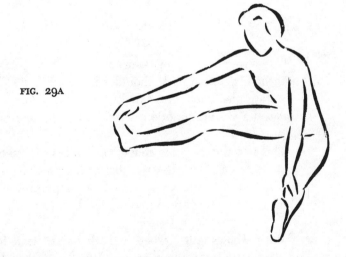

FIG. 30

Cross your feet again tailor-fashion, elbows clasped in both hands, and arms at shoulder level. (Fig. 30)

Rotate the body very slightly from the base of the spine in a weaving motion. Clockwise then counterclockwise.

This is a watch-spring movement—the action should be as delicate (and effective) as that of the finest Swiss timepiece. You are building up your most important area and storing future well-being.

With elbows still clasped in both hands, lean forward to touch the right elbow to the right knee, then the left elbow to the left knee. After a few times, change the position of the legs by recrossing them.

This action causes the body to sway from side to side in a seesaw motion.

94

Inhale when at center—exhale when the elbow touches the knee.

This movement can be increased by touching the elbow to the floor in front of you, first with one elbow and then with the other one. Do this a few times, recrossing the legs, and then try it with both elbows simultaneously. Breathing correctly is most important.

Sit on the floor with the legs outstretched, comfortably apart, and the hands on the toes. Inhale and flex the right leg; exhale as you extend it; then do the same with the left leg. Continue this up and down movement rhythmically. (Fig. 31)

First flex then extend both legs at the same time. It's fun!

FIG. 31

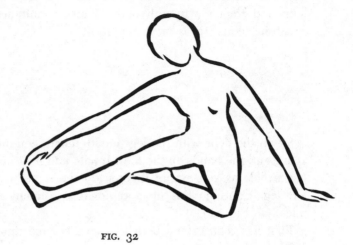

FIG. 32

Sit on the floor; extend the right leg and bring the left foot in along the inner right thigh. Support yourself with the left hand on the floor to the side. Place the right hand on the right knee and then touch the toes; bring the hand back to the knee and go forward again to the toes. (Fig. 32) After a few times, repeat the movement on the left side. The body moves forwards and backwards rhythmically with a strong flexion in the wrist of the supporting hand.

With a little patience and practice you will see how gradually you develop greater neuromuscular control and more and more freedom in the areas that have been restricted. In the beginning, be a little indulgent; let your body set its own limits; let it establish its own tempo; respect its wisdom.

All these exercises affect the unused inner thigh muscles. And such is the body's intelligence, that if you extend the leg too far and too soon, the knee will jump right up to give the alert that you are getting beyond your limits. This is the moment for reassurance.

> Sit on the floor with the legs outstretched, comfortably apart. Place the right hand on the right leg as far toward the foot as you can, comfortably.
> Place the left hand on the right knee.
> Inhale and raise the knee.
> Exhale and press it down gently but firmly on the floor.
> Repeat several times; then transfer the hand positions to the other leg and do the movement in the same way. Continue a few times alternating the legs, then place one hand on each knee and continue the up and down movement simultaneously. Now place the hands on the toes and repeat the same movement. As both knees rise on the inhalation and lower on the exhalation, it feels as though the knees themselves were doing the breathing. The tightened areas under the knees become relaxed and "giving." These caressing movements induce a sense of security.

Good results may take a little time. But once the body realizes that it is being taken care of, it gains its own confidence, and these leg movements can be done with impunity. No longer is there an involuntary reflex knee action. It is almost as if the knee had responded—if you love me, I will love you—and the exercise is accomplished with ease. Not in a narcissistic manner—but as a demonstration of the body's co-operation with correct treatment.

97

Sit as in Fig. 32. Swing the left arm up and over the body to clasp the right foot with both hands. (Fig. 33) Return the left arm to its original position and repeat. Change the leg position and do the same movement on the other side.

You may not succeed fully in the first attempts; go only as far as you can without straining. In these lessons everyone learns to make the best use of whatever equipment he has. You will be delighted with what the practice of these exercises can do for you.

FIG. 33

Sit on the floor with the soles of the feet together and take hold of the toes of the right foot with the right hand. Clasp the left ankle with the left hand.

Without releasing the toes from the right hand, slide the leg out to the side as far as you can on the floor, then bring it back to the original position. Repeat this several times. Then shift the position to the other side and do the same.

Then, with the soles of the feet together, take hold of the toes of both feet with both hands, and slide them out and in toward the crotch simultaneously. Repeat a few times.

When the soles of the feet are together again, clasp the left ankle with the left hand for leverage, hold the right

FIG. 34

toes with the right hand, and raise and extend the leg slightly off the floor. (Fig. 34) Repeat a few times.

Extend the leg higher off the floor as far out to the side as you can without strain; then flex and extend it several times. Do the same with the left leg.

Alternate the leg extensions.

Now extend both legs upward at the same time. Be sure that you have clearance all around you when you try this movement. In the beginning, you may lose your balance. This movement is only added for those who may enjoy a little challenge. You are not expected to be able to do it on the first attempts. So do not strain or force, and maybe sometime soon you, too, will master it.

One day a professional woman golfer came to me, strapped in a heavy surgical corset. She had had to give up golfing due to the agony in her back. She had tried all kinds of treatments, and was becoming convinced that her pain was incurable or that some dread operation might have to be performed.

After following some of my routines, she found that my exercises, especially those for straightening the spine and strengthening the lower back muscles, had given her more relief than anything she had ever done before. In a few months, she was able to discard her steel corset and was soon back again on the golf course, glorying in her improvement and talking of a miracle. She never wore the contraption again.

Of course, there was nothing miraculous in the change.

The last five sectors of the spinal column are unattached to the rib cage. These are the lumbar vertebrae, the center of so much misery—slipped discs, sacroiliac troubles and sciatica. Muscular strands hold these bones in place and move them when required. And muscles must be kept in toned, elastic condition for good performance.

The human structure is organized to maintain itself at its best from the beginning of life to the end, providing we understand its mechanism well enough to recognize its needs. Those lumbar muscles need exercise—*nothing excessive or misdirected*, but gentle *persuasive action* conforming wholly to their natural function. Misuse or maladjustment causes infinite pain. In almost every case muscles respond to corrective activity, no matter at what age you begin, just as a broken bone knits, or a wound heals. It is just a question of helping them back to good normal use.

For those who spend long hours in a low-slung sports car (sitting as though in a rowboat!) you will find the swaying, circling, rotating exercises most comforting and excellent for relieving fatigue in the lower back. You can give yourself a little treatment as you stop at a red light. Inhale and exhale deeply which will draw in the abdominal wall; rotate right-to-left and left-to-right from the base of the spine a few times, before speeding on your way. You will feel like a different person on arrival.

Sit with the knees drawn up about 18 inches apart. Place the hands slightly behind you, palms flat on the floor. (Fig. 35)

Press the knees forwards, lifting the buttocks slightly. Be sure to keep the feet flat. Sit back on the floor again. Repeat several times.

Center the activity in the middle of the body, till you get into a rocking action.

FIG. 35

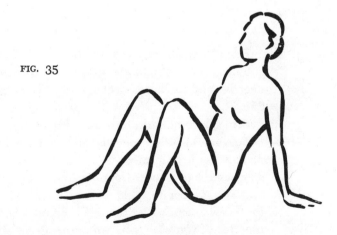

FIG. 35A

Propel yourself forward in a handwalk. (Fig. 35A)

Shift your weight forward as one arm swings up and over beyond the knees, when your balance permits. (Fig. 35B)

Bring the other arm forward. (Fig. 35C)

To your surprise, you will find you are in a squatting position with your knees wide apart, your feet flat on the floor, and your hands dropping limply before you. If you find you are comfortable enough in this position, hold it for a few seconds—the time of holding will increase with practice. If you wish, you can return to the sitting position and try it again, otherwise: lean forward to support yourself on your hands; push up slowly with your seat; raise the torso and lo and behold! you are in an easy, upright position—ready to . . .

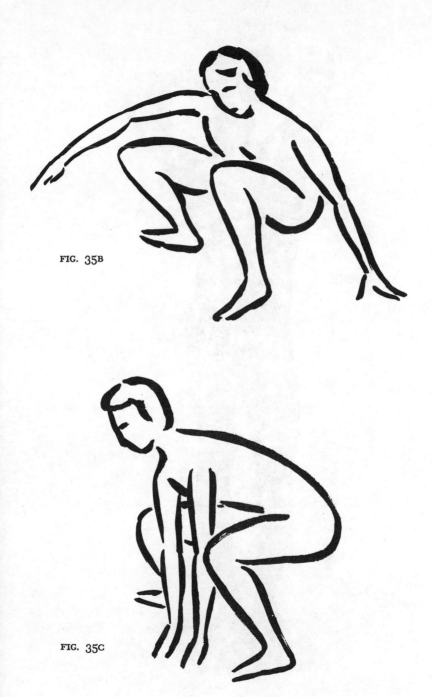

FIG. 35B

FIG. 35C

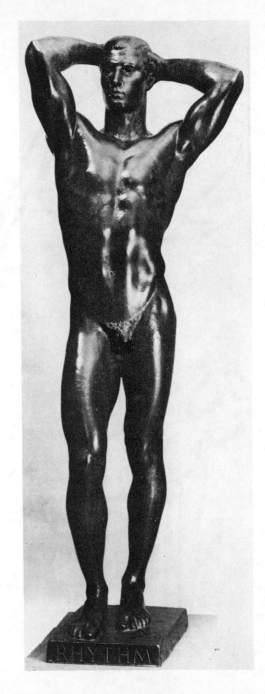

FIG. 35D "RHYTHM" BRONZE BY ARTHUR LEE. *Collection of the Whit-
ney Museum of American Art, New York.*

5 Stand and Face the World

In the preceding chapters I have outlined exercises to release pressures by stretching and strengthening the muscles of the lower back and spine, the inner thighs and the abdominal wall; and to bring them into condition for their best performance. Now we are going to make use of these movements in the standing position, for of all body positions the *standing posture* is the most demanding and the one we use most frequently.

All kinds of professional and domestic work keep us on our feet as we move around the house doing endless chores.

Some of us have been known to take a walk deliberately! But whether we loiter on a shopping spree, a sightseeing tour, or a round of cocktail parties, a great deal of life is spent standing.

Good posture, as we have noted, depends on proper

breathing, correct distribution of weight, and relaxed use of the long back muscles, the buttocks, and muscles of the shoulder blades. All these have to be brought into use unconsciously so as to hold us up comfortably, without rigidity or strain.

Assume an easy standing position, feet parallel about 5 inches apart, and heels anchored. (Fig. 36)

Roll the ankles towards each other to help "feel" your weight along the inner margins of the foot from heel to ball. This is the line of the arch that carries the whole body and is your foundation for proper alignment and balance.

Since it is of extreme importance that, at no time during any of the movements, should the shoulders rise and fall in breathing—*imagine* that you are holding a heavy bucket of water in each hand. Resist the downward pull on the body—merely allow the weight of the buckets to keep your shoulders down. Your head—that fifteen-pound load you tote everywhere—braces itself in counterbalance to the downward pull of the weight in your hands, and your chin rises slightly.

Take a full breath. Although the rib cage expands and the chest rises, those heavy buckets keep your shoulders down.

Exhale completely. The abdomen draws in, the chest rises high and the chin only slightly, *but* the shoulders remain down and motionless.

Carefully place the heavy buckets on the floor and come back to standing empty-handed, with the arms and hands free and relaxed.

Take a full breath, as your rib cage expands and your chest rises; exhale slowly and completely. Now your abdomen is in, your chest is high, your head is well-placed, and your shoulders are down. Swing your arms freely forwards and backwards to release them. *Without thinking about good posture, you have achieved it!*

With the heels well-anchored to the floor and the arms hanging freely at the sides, allow the body to sway forward without any change in the position of the head or shoulders. (Fig. 37) The line of the body should be kept absolutely perpendicular; be careful not to break at the small of the back as the body balances itself forward. Hold this position as long as you can before shifting your

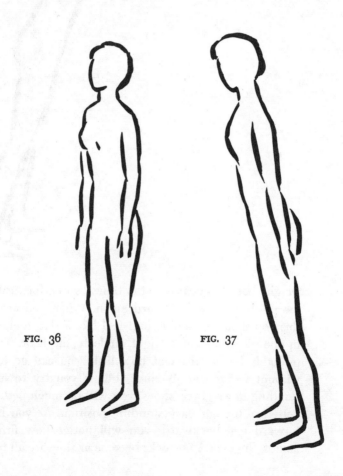

FIG. 36   FIG. 37

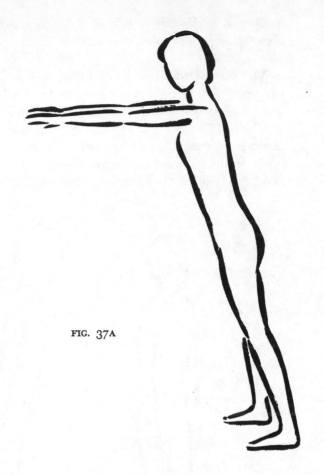

FIG. 37A

weight back. Repeat several times; sway forward—hold the position—then backward again. When you are doing this you should resemble and feel like a slat; inclined, all in one piece, and at a slight angle to the floor. You will probably be surprised at how little you can go forward without losing your balance, but if you try to imagine standing in weighted shoes, you will do much better.

Return to your easy standing position. As you balance forward and backward, you will notice how firm your ankles, thighs and buttocks become as they are all brought into activity. Without specifically exercising them, they are getting a thorough workout.

For release, raise one knee and then the other one, in a high stepping fashion.

Sway forward and backward a few times and hold the forward stance. Slowly raise the right arm to shoulder level in front of you; then raise the left one parallel to it. (Fig. 37A)

Bring one arm back behind your body as far as you can (Fig. 37B) then alternate with the other arm. Continue rhythmically. As one arm comes forward, the other one goes back as though you were resisting the wind or swimming in air.

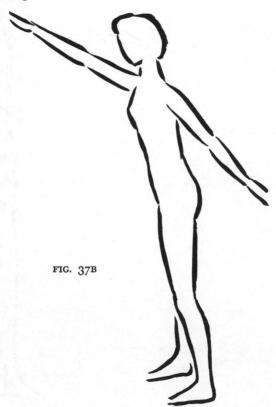

FIG. 37B

Sway forward again, heels well-anchored, arms down at the sides, and head well-placed. Bring one arm forward to shoulder level; keep it extended in front of you; then bring the other one parallel to it. Take a full breath. Exhale as you raise both arms overhead and bring the backs of the hands together, at the same time shifting your full weight back over the feet.

Inhale as the arms flow wide apart and slowly outward to shoulder level.

Exhale as they rise again and the hands meet back-to-back overhead. After repeating this a few times, you experience a feeling of total exultation!

FIG. 37C

Assume an easy standing position, arms down at the sides, and feet parallel, about 10 or 12 inches apart. Rise on your toes as high as you can, then lower the heels alternately. Repeat this a few times in an easy rhythm. Then increase the tempo and the knee flexion. This may not be exactly like mountain climbing, but the effect on your leg muscles is somewhat similar.

Raise both arms straight up overhead, close to your ears. Come up on your toes, heels off the floor. Lower the right arm forward as the right heel returns to the floor. Raise the right arm and your right heel, as you lower the left arm, and the left heel returns to the floor. (Fig. 38) Continue in an unbroken rhythm.

As the movement progresses the arms and feet all move at the same time like a puppet on a string. When you are fully in the rhythm of this movement, you forget yourself completely and it becomes automatic. Adding a little gusto increases the fun as your entire body, including every part of your feet, goes gaily swinging up and down. But more than the fun is the delicious articulation in the arches and the ankles; and the loosening up of the tight cords and muscles across the top of the feet, which also releases accumulated nerve tensions at the back of the neck and shoulders.

Stand with both arms raised overhead, close to the ears; raise your heels off the floor and come up on your toes.

Replace the right heel on the floor; then raise it as you place the left heel on the floor. Continue until an alternating rhythm is established.

Now as you raise the right heel, reach higher with the right arm and feel it drawing up from the hip. (Fig. 38A) Do the same on the left side. Continue this alternating rhythm.

This synchronized foot-knee-shoulder-arm action lifts

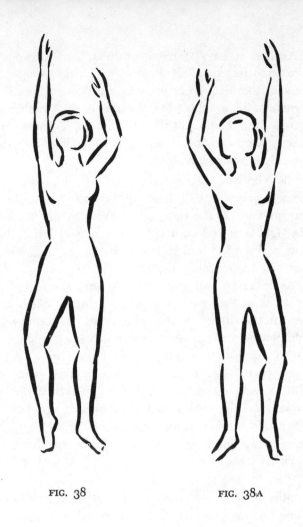

FIG. 38   FIG. 38A

you out of your hips, almost out of yourself, and gives you
a feeling of weightlessness, as though you were floating
away.

Look up at the ceiling as you continue, and you will
actually feel that you are ascending, climbing higher and
higher. It is like "reaching for the stars."

This is one of the best ways to prepare for climbing
stairs. Next time you ascend a flight, remember to remain

elegantly tall, with an unbroken line of the torso and head and a smooth, graceful shifting of your weight through the hips; you will attract admiration from anyone behind you.

Stand with a free and easy posture, arms and shoulders relaxed, and feet parallel about 10 inches apart. Rise on to the toes of both feet; then lower the right foot *only* and tap the floor with the heel three times. Now do the same with the left foot. Continue in a smooth and easy rhythm. This movement sets up its own vibration through the entire body. By accelerating the tapping, you can increase the vibration. By tapping more slowly, you reduce it.

Now try rising on to the toes of both feet and tap the floor with both heels at the same time in continuous succession. Very gradually increase the speed of heel-to-floor action. Interesting, isn't it?

As you can see here is another demonstration of your own built-in equipment. If it is vibration that you want, to loosen and relax you from head to toe, all you have to do is use your own apparatus, which you can set at any speed you desire. You realize now that you have always had a built-in vibrator, but until this very moment, perhaps, you did not know where to find the switch.

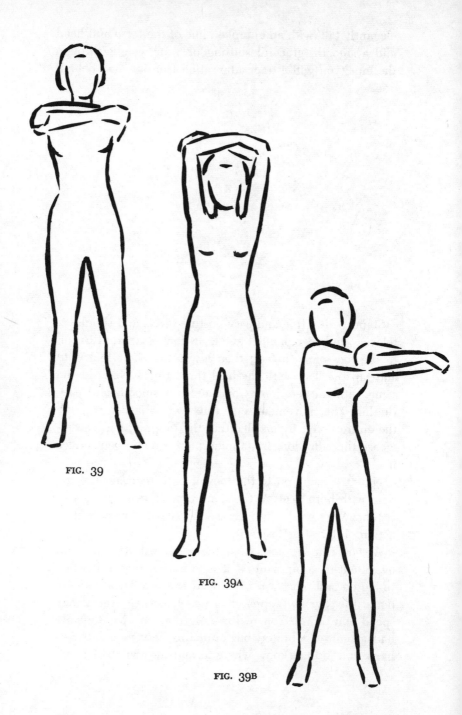

FIG. 39

FIG. 39A

FIG. 39B

Stand at ease with the feet turned out about 20 inches apart. Place the hands on the elbows, then raise the arms to shoulder level. (Fig. 39) Take a deep breath and exhale as you raise the arms overhead. (Fig. 39A) Inhale as the arms return to shoulder level. Repeat several times.

With the arms at shoulder level and the hands still clasped on the elbows, take a deep breath. Exhale as you extend the arms as far to the right as you can and let the head flow toward the left side. (Fig. 39B) Inhale as the head and arms return to center. Exhale as you extend the arms to the left side and the head to the right side. Continue a few times. Notice how rhythmically your breathing flows in and out from center.

With the feet wider apart and the hands still clasped on the elbows, flex the knees and let the body drop forwards. Tap the right elbow on the right knee and shift immediately to the left side to tap the left elbow on the

FIG. 39C

left knee. (Fig. 39C) Continue several times, alternating from side to side.

Lower the body further, aiming to touch the right elbow to the right ankle, and then the left elbow to the left ankle.

Do not alter the position of the body. Unfold the arms. Bounce your seat up and down as the hands raise and lower to the floor. (Fig. 39D)

Then swing the arms forward and backward with impetus from the seat, in a free and easy rhythm.

These movements set up a turning and a twisting through the middle of the body. Development of the muscles in this area of the midriff and of the back slim the waistline and keep the weight of the body off the hip joints, allowing them increased freedom of movement. Care of this central part of the body develops beauty, strength, and better balance.

116

With the feet 10 or 12 inches apart and the arms at the sides, "breathe" the arms out and up to shoulder level, with the wrists leading and hands limp. Exhale as the arms sink back to the sides. Repeat 3 or 4 times.

Inhale and bring the arms up again to shoulder level. Exhale as they rise overhead and the backs of the hands come lightly together. Inhale and bring the arms down to shoulder level. Raise and lower them from there in fluttering gestures several times. You will find that as the arms rise, the entire body is lifted out of itself and creates the sensation of flying.

With the legs 10 or 12 inches apart, raise the arms to an upward V position. (Fig. 40)

Rise on the right toe and raise the entire right side of the torso. Carry the right arm over to the left side so that the palm of the right hand flows over to the palm of the left hand. (Fig. 40A) The right arm returns to the open V position before the weight is shifted to the left toe. Do the same on the left side. Continue until the shifting is done with such ease and rhythm that the whole movement is a continuous flow from one side to the other.

This exercise is the same as the one above, except that instead of bringing the palms together, you allow the fingers of the right hand to flow over those of the left hand. Do the same on the left side. (Fig. 40B)

These extensions from the tip of the toe to the tip of the finger overhead are the longest of which the body is capable. If you remember to breathe in when your arms are in the open V position and to exhale as they move from side to side, you will experience the great joy and satisfaction of releasing from deep within you, movement that flows out and beyond into endless space.

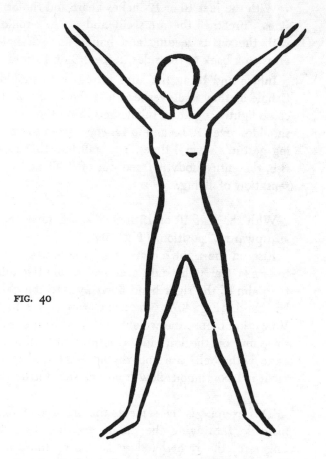

FIG. 40

A few repetitions of most exercises is sufficient. Remember that what is most important is the *way* you do them, not how long. The body only accepts with advantage a certain amount of exercise at any one time. To exercise every day, if only for a short time, has the most beneficial effect. Once the balance and the rhythmic flow of the movements have been established, you can do them as long as you wish without any possibility of overdoing.

You have now become aware that the use of your body is an ever-growing experience; that not only physical devel-

FIG. 40A

FIG. 40B

opment, but emotional release as well, is more easily accomplished with harmonious, rhythmical movement. These

lessons have provided you with a new concept of self-development.

Now quietly bring the palms of your hands together and gently raise the hands as you lower the forehead to touch them. With this gesture of infinite grace, you give thanks for the blessed instrument that is *you* and *yours* to perfect.

6 Zen and Body Dynamics

As you do these exercises, you begin to see the connection between your physical work and its underlying principles.

Until you have tried the former and practiced breathing, rolling and stretching; until you have experienced what Body Dynamics is doing to your physique, it is pointless to speak of other matters, or tell you much about the Zen Way which influences it.

Nor do I intend to go into this in detail. My small volume is no place for philosophy. Many may not be interested in it at all; and those who care may read for themselves any book suggested in the appendix. But even for the uninitiated, the work becomes more compelling and significant as its relationship to Zen becomes clearer.

My aim is to help you develop into a healthy, vital and interesting person.

Bodies are like electric batteries, full of mysterious power which is ready and waiting for release. I help you to tap this latent force, utilizing everything within you. Unless this power finds an outlet and is brought into operation, it withers away. Or it can become warped, cramped and distorted, and express itself in abnormal ways.

Zen, too, liberates energies which are properly and naturally stored in us. It points the way to greater personal freedom, brings self-knowledge, and provides that crucial outlet which saves us from crippling inhibitions and frustrations.

Many of us are blind to the fact that all the necessary requisites for happiness are in ourselves; among them are the faculties which enable us to understand and love our neighbors.

Ignoring this causes much tension and misfortune.

Zen helps to open our "third eye," that hitherto undreamed-of region closed to us by woeful ignorance. The essence of Zen is *acquiring a new viewpoint*—of things in general and of ourselves in particular. It is an *intuitive* survey, in contradistinction to logical understanding; it is a flashing of a new truth into consciousness. In many ways it resembles the enlightenment or "inner light" which inspired and guided early Quakers. And since, in the land of its adoption—Japan—its significance and meaning closely influence artistic expression —in the arts of dancing, fencing and archery—it can readily be understood why Body Dynamics profits by its special teaching.

The idea of Zen is to catch life as it flows, to move with it, without arresting its flow and to feel *at one* with it. For this, no words or discussion are necessary. To define is often to falsify or destroy. The method of Zen is to excite and inspire.

"When the sun rises, the whole world dances with joy and everybody's heart is filled with bliss," say Zen masters. And if Zen is to be comprehended, it must be taken hold of right here, without reservation. Its peace of mind, too, "passeth understanding."

A form of mysticism, then, you say? Inevitably, since Zen is a keynote of Oriental culture. But it is not an isolated religious experience; there is no doctrinal teaching, or formal spiritual program. It is intensely practical. It has its systematic discipline, it is true, but also its down-to-earth side. Zen is your everyday mind, filling everyday needs.

One of its characteristics is its "secret virtue"—practicing good without thought of reward. It emphasizes the desirability of detachment from material things. It involves, primarily, a letting go, particularly of self. In Zen there is no sense of "I am doing this," but rather an inner realization that "this is happening through me," or "it is doing this for me." The consciousness of *self* is the greatest hindrance to the proper execution of all physical action. Spontaneity is lost when body muscles are hampered by an awareness of their functioning.

This absence of self-consciousness is basic in Body Dynamics. A strictly noninterfering mental attitude is one of its most vital components. Movements follow each other in a continuous flow without prompting by the conscious mind. They resemble the smooth passage of a boat gliding down a stream. In this lack of conscious effort lie their beauty and efficacy. This is what is really meant by "poetry of motion."

Zen teachers speak of "the mental attitude of immoveable wisdom." This wisdom comes only after much practical training. Its "immovability" is no happenstance. If one really wishes to be master of an art, technical knowledge alone is not enough. One must transcend mere technique to acquire that "artless art" which is the by-product of the unconscious. To be immobile, in the Zen sense, does not mean to be lifeless, stiff, or motionless. It is the concentration of energy at a given focus—as at the axis of a wheel—instead of dispersal in scattered activities. Only the uncontrolled mind wastes energy on a thousand distracting worries. Zen counsels economizing forces and holding strength in reserve. This typifies the Zen paradox of action which is no action and the moveable and immoveable which are one and the same.

Reflection on some of these matters gives you a satisfying background for further physical work. It furnishes an incentive for the attainment of an innate self-control, which is highly necessary and valuable in today's world.

With mind attuned to body, and a relaxation springing from inner resources, you find yourself in better balance. You discover the meaning as well as the value of "being centered." Your proper alignment established, your stance and posture are corrected automatically. Something is "happening through you," as the oriental masters teach.

Body Dynamics brings you into the state where you naturally assume good form in all you do, and to a consciousness of the unchanging values of beauty.

With practice, these standing, sitting and reclining exercises imperceptibly become part of you. The fascination of the movements themselves exert their own influence, once they become part of your daily routine. Without too much conscious direction, they "take over," and your response is an immediate exhilaration. The results, too, are speedily visible. You walk with a light rhythmic gait as though you were hardly walking at all. So beautifully motionless are your head and shoulders that you feel as if you were sitting in a ricksha, carried along by its motion instead of your own.

Co-ordinated movement like this, springs from the assimilation of all you have learned; the unconscious and the subconscious both contributing a part.

You have learned to efface your ego so that consciousness of self is subordinated to concentrating on the task in hand. You have found a fundamental unity of body and purpose

FIG. 41   RUTH ST. DENIS . . . *"the unchanging values of beauty."*

from which a new inner harmony materializes in action on the physical plane.

On this plane, with your newly-acquired body flow, you interpret and exemplify the very spirit of Zen with its insistence on *moving with life* without trying to arrest and interrupt its flow. You, too, go ahead with your work, without dwelling unduly upon your own reactions to it.

Rhythm has become a vital factor in your existence, extending far beyond the exercises you do. In time you will even recognize your remaining tensions as a rewarding experience, accepting and affirming them as an integral part of life's pendulum swing; just as darkness is the complement of light, and the sun is both the destroyer and creator of living matter. You will take obstacles in your stride, making them stepping stones to achievement.

So a husband or a wife forgets a birthday or an anniversary! Fill the house with flowers and thank each other for *understanding,* one of the greatest gifts on earth. This is just a shift in your point of view. But how important!

By discovering and centering your physical forces, you have established a oneness and a sense of integration that frees your body to create its own well-being. You have brought its skeletal framework into a balanced state wherein the various parts function naturally. In doing this you fulfill Zen's aim, too, which is to release the mind from having to think about the body.

Zen's principle of "going right ahead" in life as in all art without wasted energy, is also paralleled by your own economy of motion in all you do. A harmonious muscular system cuts out dispersed effort. It is free from all that is superfluous or nonessential. The good walker, as you have seen, uses just the right amount of energy to propel himself forward; not a jot more.

If you fear that Zen's acceptance of all things may tend

to justify every act, that its all-inclusive pervasiveness may spread its message too thin, then do not forget the rigid discipline observed in Zen communities. No society can long endure without moral training. The age-old duration of Chinese and Japanese civilizations—compared with many in the West—must be attributed primarily to the self-discipline of its teaching.

Students of Body Dynamics, do not, it is true, adopt the techniques of Zen. But they can take from it its "moment of truth," the flash of enlightenment, which is not unlike a sudden conversion, and in which all distinction of "I" and "not I" are set aside.

In a sense this can be our shield in a world that is "too much with us."

As gadgets and traffic continue to multiply, the techniques for externalizing life become daily more blatant and distracting. Now that technological ingenuity has put limitless power into man's hands, and now that this modern fragmented creature possesses the ability to blow himself and his planet to pieces, it is perhaps common sense to shift the gaze from externals and look inward.

Your hour of physical development can be your hour of awakening and recovery of the strength that is dormant in us all.

SELECTED BIBLIOGRAPHY

Suzuki, D. T. *Introduction to Zen Buddhism.* London: Rider and Company, 1949.

———. *Zen Buddhism. Selected Writings of D. T. Suzuki.* Garden City: Anchor Books, Doubleday and Company, 1956.

Watts, Alan. *The Spirit of Zen.* London: John Murray, 1936. New York: Grove Press, 1959.

Herrigel, Eugene. *Zen in the Art of Archery.* New York: Pantheon Books, 1953.

SOME COMMENTS ON BODY DYNAMICS

"A valuable and delightful guide to fuller living is Gertrude Enelow's *Body Dynamics.*"

—James T. McCay, author of *The Management of Time*

"After five weeks' hospitalization for a broken arm, my mother was told that at her age (over 70) she must resign herself to its painful uselessness. Body Dynamics restored its mobility and improved her whole outlook on life."

—Irma Morgenthau (Mrs. Hans Morganthau)

"It was a privilege to be a guest at one of Mrs. Enelow's classes last Spring and observe this new concept in body dynamics, which was a complete revelation to me. The positive enjoyment on the part of the students made it a wonderful experience."

—Mrs. Benjamin Fain, Executive Director,
The Adult Education Council of Greater Chicago

"My back pain was so severe and constant that some expert opinion held it might be remedied only by drastic surgery. Therapy gave temporary relief, but it was a nuisance to go constantly for treatments. Foreign travel, far from good therapy, was sometimes a misery. Then I discovered Body Dynamics. Now I can usually relieve back pains myself . . . which is a great joy."

—Margaret Buchen, Vice-President of an
international advertising agency

"I have highly recommended Gertrude Enelow's Body Dynamics for years."

—Joseph Mueller, M.D.